Poetic Lives:
Shelley

Poetic Lives:
Shelley

Daniel Hahn

ET REMOTISSIMA PROPE

Poetic Lives
Published by Hesperus Press Limited
4 Rickett Street, London sw6 1ru
www.hesperuspress.com

First published by Hesperus Press Limited, 2009

Designed and typeset by Fraser Muggeridge studio
Printed in Jordan by Al-Khayyam Printing Press

ISBN: 978-1-84391-300-9

Contents

It's natural to think of Percy Bysshe Shelley as a writer from a world that is very far away. He is, after all, a character we find in the realm of mad King George, from the world of Schubert's Trout Quintet, of Whigs in Parliament and wigs at court, of European struggles for independence and revolution and the Emperor Napoleon – a name from a time that belongs firmly to history. But in truth, it's not so long since he was drifting on the Thames in his boat composing a poem, or struggling to publish some troublesome radical pamphlet. Two centuries ago Shelley was still just a schoolboy, a difficult teenager causing trouble for his teachers and his parents, his writing life not yet begun. His granddaughter Eliza, the oldest of his grandchildren, saw the sinking of the *Titanic*, the First World War, the Great Depression; she died the year Ted Hughes was born. Our connection to Shelley's world is not as distant as it may seem. And if you go today to Warnham in West Sussex, just a couple of miles north-west of Horsham, you'll find the house where he was born, Field Place, still standing.

While yet a boy...

Field Place is an attractive old estate house, Tudor with many recent additions, set in a good-sized park and farm. It's a simple, solid house, a broad, two-storey front backing onto an old stone courtyard. Field Place had been in the Shelley family since the early eighteenth century; Shelley's great-uncle John had lived there, during which time he developed the American garden, sequoias and all, which is still there today. When John died childless in 1790, the house passed to his brother, Bysshe, who waived his right to it in favour of his son, Timothy, who would move in at once with his new bride, a local girl called Elizabeth Pilfold. Timothy, already in his late thirties, had just been made MP for Horsham, thanks to his alliance with his neighbour, the influential Whig politician the Duke of Norfolk.

Timothy and Elizabeth married in October 1791 at West Grinstead, West Sussex, and the new bride gave birth to the couple's first child on 4th August the following year. He was named Percy Bysshe, after a great-uncle (and the Percys of Northumberland, to whom an aunt was dimly related) and his paternal grandfather.

The year of Shelley's birth, 1792, was also the year that Mary Wollstonecraft's *A Vindication of the Rights of Woman* appeared; the previous year, Thomas Paine had invited a sedition trial upon himself for the ideas expressed in his newly published *Rights of Man*; a year later, across the Channel, France's Reign of Terror would begin. These were the convulsions of societies and nations that – understandably, perhaps – would form the backdrop for the most dynamic years of English Romantic poetry, the work of writers as politically radical as they were revolutionaries in their art. Writers, in other words, like Percy Bysshe Shelley.

Percy Bysshe Shelley would be the eldest of six children – with four younger sisters and one brother. The baptism of this first boy, always known by his family as Bysshe – who would in his time be one of the most notorious of the nation's atheists – was recorded in the Parish Register on 7th September. A facsimile of the page (with 'Bysshe' misspelled and corrected) is on display at St Margaret's church at Warnham today.

The young Shelley was a good-natured, attractive boy, popular in the family (especially among his many doting sisters), and with the servants and the local workers. From his earliest childhood it was clear that he would be an enthusiastic reader, working his way through his father's library, and an equally enthusiastic talker, entertaining his younger siblings with lively tales. His father Timothy approved at least of the former of these pastimes, the avid reading; he expected his eldest son to study hard and make a fine scholar of himself.

The boy's education would be a demanding, disciplined one. He was sent first, at six years old, to a local school at Warnham run by the Reverend Evan Edwards, a Welsh curate. Then in 1802 (the year his father became MP for Shoreham), he moved on to Syon House, a small academy for some sixty pupils at Isleworth, on the Thames just west of London. He would be under the tutelage of the master Dr Greenlaw. In his eccentric Shelley biography, Edmund Blunden would comment that, 'The master, Dr Greenlaw, was a Scot; which assures us that the subjects taught – Latin, Greek, French, writing, arithmetic, geography, the elements of astronomy – would be taught accurately.' Shelley himself, meanwhile, would describe him mildly as 'a man of rather liberal opinions'.

Shelley's cousin Thomas Medwin, who preceded him at the school, described the young boy who arrived that autumn: 'He was, as a schoolboy, exceedingly shy, bashful, and reserved – indeed, though peculiarly gentle, and elegant and refined in his manners, he never entirely got rid of his diffidence – and who would have wished he should? With the characteristic of the genius, he was ever modest, humble, and prepared to acknowledge merit, wherever he found it.'

But the new boy was homesick at Syon House, as his exercise-book doodles of Field Place testify. And he was cruelly bullied by the other boarders:

> This place was a perfect hell to Shelley; his pure and virgin mind was shocked by the language and manners of his new companions; but, though forced to be *with* them, he was not *of* them. Methinks I see him now, pacing, with rapid strides, a favourite remote spot of the playground – generally alone… Tyranny generally produces tyranny in common minds – not so in Shelley. Doubtless much of his hatred of oppression may be attributed to what he saw and suffered at this school.

Shelley took what refuge he could in reading; in particular, seeking out tales of the supernatural – for which he would long retain a taste – as he described, years later, when he came to write his 'Hymn to Intellectual Beauty':

> *While yet a boy I sought for ghosts, and sped*
> *Through many a listening chamber, cave and ruin,*
> *And starlight wood, with fearful steps pursuing*
> *Hopes of high talk with the departed dead.*
> *I called on poisonous names with which our youth is fed;*
> *I was not heard – I saw them not –*
> *When musing deeply on the lot*
> *Of life, at that sweet time when winds are wooing*

> *All vital things that wake to bring*
> *News of birds and blossoming, –*
> *Sudden, thy shadow fell on me;*
> *I shrieked, and clasped my hands in ecstasy!*

But the unhappy child did not remain long at Syon House. In the summer of 1804, he would be moved further west, to one of the most distinguished of all educational establishments. In September, not long after his twelfth birthday, the Windsor coach took the young Percy Bysshe Shelley to Eton College. Early nineteenth-century Eton, under Headmaster Dr Goodall ('whose temper, character and conduct corresponded precisely with his name'), was a prestigious place, whose recent alumni included the Whig politician Charles James Fox and the dandy Beau Brummel. Shelley was, one assumes, expected to be proud of the privilege to attend.

Under the ever-benign Goodall, and Shelley's own house-master, the rigorous Mr Hexter – an army type – Eton might have been a promising place for young Shelley to develop his hungry scientific curiosity and demonstrate his great intellectual abilities. Yet it was neither a happy nor a nurturing place for the boy. The bullying that he had suffered at Syon House continued here: 'The Shelley! Shelley! Shelley! which was thundered in the cloisters was but too often accompanied by practical jokes – such as knocking his books from under his arm, seizing them as he stooped to recover them, pulling and tearing his clothes… The result was… a paroxysm of anger which made his eyes flash like a tiger's.'

Eton was, wrote Medwin, 'a new and better world: but Shelley's was a spirit that ill brooked restraint, or, in his words, he cared to "learn little that his tyrants knew or taught".' He was first dubbed 'Mad Shelley' here; later he would earn another, riskier nickname (but one given him with something like awe): the Eton Atheist. Naturally a boy averse to all kinds of exerted authority, he was vehemently opposed to the system of fagging, against which he revolted (without much effect, as it turned out, since the system was not abolished at Eton until the 1980s).

A schoolfriend from young Master Shelley's Eton days, Walter Halliday, would later write, 'He was not made to endure the rough and boisterous pastime at Eton, and his shy and gentle nature was glad to escape far away to muse over strange fancies, for his mind was reflective and teeming with thought...'

But there were also more positive aspects to his experience at Eton. He made friends, so he had people to talk to (and argue with – a great pleasure of his); and to walk with too, for this countryside boy did love to walk, alone or accompanied, in the area around the school, around Windsor Great Park, considering (or debating) his big interests as he went.

These interests were rapidly broadening, and deepening, as he began to read richly on a range of subjects and to question, to want to understand, to subject scientific theories to scientific proof. The best-known anecdote to illustrate the pursuits of his enquiring mind sees Shelley experimenting with a little electricity-generating machine, and deciding to demonstrate it to friends by wiring it up to a metal doorknob. But then a master on the far side of the door began to wonder what the commotion was about in there, and made towards the room, reached for the door handle...

'Certainly he was not happy at Eton,' Halliday continued, 'for his was a disposition that needed especial personal superintendence, to watch, cherish, and direct all his noble aspirations, and the remarkable tenderness of his heart.' And such superintendence he did indeed receive. For one of the few benefits to come to Shelley from his Eton years was his friendship with Dr James Lind, a retired physician, a well-travelled and widely read old man who would be a sort of mentor to the young scholar's intellectual curiosity and ambition.

Shelley studied hard, as he was expected to – there were still hopes for him to become an excellent classical scholar – not only dedicating himself to reading and to his Greek and Latin composition but also working on translations, to prize-winning effect; but his pursuits were not all quite this erudite, or this pleasing to his masters. For Shelley at this time was acquiring a taste for reading of a lower brow, too, devouring the romances and ghost stories so popular at the time – and which would be a significant influence on his first substantial piece of prose writing, *Zastrozzi*, published in 1810.

Zastrozzi was a short Gothic novel, wildly over-dramatic and catering to the most popular of tastes, which earned him a massive £40. His creative life in 1809 was not limited to this, however; he was also working with his cousin Medwin on a poem of the Wandering Jew, and a novel, *The Nightmare* (which no longer survives). He was collaborating too with his sister Elizabeth on *Original Poetry by Victor and Cazire*, a collection of generally rather poor poems including verses to one 'Harriet' (whom we shall meet shortly), which would be published at Worthing the following year. Thanks to the generosity of Shelley's indulgent grandfather Bysshe, 1,500 copies were printed; the publication of this collection, however, would leave a rather bitter taste, as it was discovered that one of the pieces included was a plagiarised poem by Matthew Lewis, author of the celebratedly lurid Gothic novel *The Monk*. The volume was immediately pulped.

Into Shelley's close circle around this time enters an individual who for a time seemed as though she might become a significant figure in his life: one Harriet Grove, his cousin. Towards the end of his time at Eton, Shelley had begun to spend increasingly long spells with Harriet, and the notion of a marriage was contemplated. Her family, it should be said, was less keen on the idea than his – she was potentially an advantageous daughter-in-law to acquire, he the sort of unreliable future son-in-law (and one with all sorts of odd ideas about things, moreover) who was perhaps best avoided by respectable folk. The marriage was not to be, and for all the apparently promising flaring of early passion between the cousins, Harriet was soon engaged to another local man, William Helyer – and Shelley seems not to have been much troubled. Or at least, while his letters occasionally describe his anguish, there is something hollow in his descriptions; it is the adolescent Romeo sighing for Rosaline, before he meets his Juliet. And like Romeo, Shelley forgot this Harriet as soon as another hoved into view...

The high road to Pandemonium...

In 1810 Shelley's Eton career drew to a close, a degree at Oxford beckoning. A bright future ahead of him, this young scholar was escorted up to University College by his father, who had, of course, been a University College man himself. Before leaving his son to embark on his Oxford career, Timothy introduced him to a bookseller-printer, a man by the name of Henry Slatter, encouraging him to indulge the new student's 'printing freaks' – the promising young man had already published *Zastrozzi*, even before leaving Eton. It would be only a few months before Shelley *père* would come to regret this encouragement.

University College, Oxford in 1810 was a bastion of history and stifling tradition, an establishment of some two hundred students under the care of Master James Griffith. Into this refined atmosphere came the wild-eyed Shelley, filling his room in the main quad with scientific experimental equipment and reading his way off the syllabus. His old electricity machine was here too, and he demonstrated it now – having learned to be wary of foolishness with doorknobs – by making his hair stand on end.

Books, boots, papers, shoes, philosophical instruments, clothes, pistols, linen, crockery, ammunition, and phials innumerable, with money, stockings, prints, crucibles, bags, and boxes, were scattered on the floor and in every place;

as if the young chemist, in order to analyse the mystery of creation, had endeavoured first to reconstruct the primeval chaos. The tables, and especially the carpet, were already stained with large spots of various hues, which frequently proclaimed the agency of fire. An electrical machine, an air-pump, the galvanic trough, a solar microscope, and large glass jars and receivers, were conspicuous amidst the mass of matter...

This description of Shelley's college room (philosophical instruments? ammunition?) comes from the writing of Thomas Jefferson Hogg, whose recollections tell us much of what we know about Shelley's Oxford days. (The brilliant depiction, incidentally, continues for paragraphs and paragraphs – an argand lamp, pieces of lemon...) This young man, a wealthy lawyer's son, had preceded Shelley to Oxford by six or seven months. Shelley's closest friend at the University, Hogg would half a century later write a *Life of Shelley* in which their university days are described with enthusiasm and colour, albeit in descriptions somewhat questionable in their accuracy. Hogg was a scholarly young man, and a bright one, who would encourage Shelley in his unconventional ideas and in his writing, which in this first Michaelmas term would include *Posthumous Fragments of Margaret Nicholson*, a collection written in collaboration with Hogg and subtitled 'being poems found amongst the Papers of that noted Female who attempted the Life of the King in 1786'. And though, as we will see later, Shelley himself was certainly no more of a monarchist than Margaret Nicholson, the poems – well described by Medwin as a 'strange half-mad volume' – are not the republican or regicidal calls to arms one might have expected, but merely a peculiar assortment of indifferently successful verse pastiches.

There were other poems written at Oxford, too, but discouraged by Hogg:

… he put the proofs into my hands. I read them twice attentively, for the poems were very short; and I told him there were some good lines, some bright thoughts but there were likewise many irregularities and incongruities. I added, that correctness was important in all compositions, but it constituted the essence of short ones; and that it surely would be imprudent to bring his little book out so hastily; and then pointed out the errors and defects.

Shelley wouldn't publish another collection of poems for a while…

Perhaps the best known episode in Hogg's recollections of this time came when he and his friend were crossing Magdalen Bridge, and Shelley, buzzing, his mind always on the big questions of Life – and always curious, and never very good at restraining himself – accosted a young mother, seized her baby and asked, 'Will your baby tell us anything about pre-existence, madam?'

Apart from his friendship with Hogg, Shelley's life at University College was not an overly sociable one, a set-up which suited him well. Cousin Medwin wrote:

Shelley, whilst at University College, formed but one friendship, and even that one was the effect of an accident. Nor did this arise from any unsocial feeling, but from an unwillingness and dislike to form acquaintances with strangers, which characterised him all his life. That stiffness and formality, and unapproachableness, which are so justly ridiculed by foreigners in Englishmen, are not confined to the great world, but begin at the University – perhaps there were no Etonians whom Shelley knew in the College – perhaps he shrunk from the idea of asking for introductions, and, entirely occupied in his pursuits and lucubrations, and always communing with himself, he knew not what solitude meant.

Oxford saw yet more and broader reading (on the curriculum and off it), yet more walks in the Oxfordshire countryside and more well-relished arguments, with Hogg and occasional others. By the Christmas holidays, Shelley had formulated arguments that would cause trouble back home, as the religious season seemed to bring out the atheist in him. Among the thirteen (thirteen!) long letters he wrote to Hogg in his few weeks back home, he wrote:

'My father wished to withdraw me from college: I would not consent to it. There lowers a terrific tempest, but I stand, as it were, on a pharos, and smile exultingly at the vain beating of the billows below...'

And 'My mother imagines me to be in the high road to Pandemonium, she fancies I want to make a deistical coterie of all my little sisters: how laughable!...'

The atheist in him was more outspoken still by the time he had returned to Oxford for his second term, in the new year of 1811.

Shelley's atheism would in one respect be consistent through his life – he would always be firm in his scepticism of the specifically Christian God, and always happy to express these doubts about His existence (or more properly, his absolute certainty of His non-existence). On this subject he is rarely, if ever, moderate.

But there was a time in his youth when he didn't deny the possibility of *any* God, and deism attracted his sympathies for a while: 'I *once* was an enthusiastic Deist, but never a Christian.' And he would often invoke some spiritual power, a spirit of nature, perhaps, not a great humanlike father-figure God but a kind of shapeless 'soul of the universe', as he called it.

His doubts about Christianity – about organised religion in general – were linked to his dislike of all authority, of course, but also to his belief in human potential, creativity, liberty; he would later write, 'The delusions of Christianity are fatal to genius and originality; they limit thought.'

As a young man devoted to logic, it was clear that this would surely be the main weapon in his attempt to argue against religion – to argue, in his words, for *The Necessity of Atheism*. This was a pamphlet he had written, with some collaboration with Hogg, and had published in Worthing. Upon returning to Oxford he decided to have it circulated among significant people he felt ought to read it. This was possibly not merely a piece of provocation – the logical arguer in Shelley genuinely wanted to challenge others to offer counter-arguments, to take him on and discuss the subject, though not everyone would see it that benignly. At the core of the case he made was the certainty that 'the senses are the source of all knowledge to the mind.' Many would disagree.

Copies of *The Necessity of Atheism* went out all over Oxford, and beyond; it had been published without his name on it, and sent with a covering letter signed with a pseudonym, but it was not hard to guess who the author might be. And when the Reverend Jocelyn Walker saw a copy in Slatter's shop the real trouble began. The Master and Dons of University College met, and the young troublemaker was called to appear before them.

The meeting took place on 25th March – Shelley had not yet completed a year at the University. Questioned about the pamphlet, he did not acknowledge his authorship of it, but nor did he deny it. He was sent out of the room. Next up was Hogg, who told his inquisitors that if any kind of punishment were to be meted out to Shelley, then he deserved a share in it himself. The two young men were expelled. The next morning they were on a coach to London.

Having been removed from Oxford, but clearly – given the cause of that removal – not being in a position to return to the bosom of his God-fearing family, Shelley decided upon London as the sensible place to go. Having first looked at other residences that didn't meet his standards, the two friends took rooms at 15 Poland Street, just east of what would soon be Regent Street; this major new boulevard, set to sweep grandly down to St James's from Regent's Park, was just being planned out as Shelley moved in down the road.

Cousin Tom Medwin was in London already, having himself left Oxford without a degree, and was now at the Temple. He was rather startled to be awoken at four o'clock one morning by his young cousin Bysshe calling out to him in his distinctive high-pitched voice that he'd been expelled, and he laughed – 'for atheism!'

Shelley's father hoped his son might be made to settle (and give up his troublesome atheist phase too, obviously) by one of two remedies – either a long trip of some kind, to Greece, perhaps, or by following him into Parliament, but neither suggestion impressed Shelley very much. His radical ideas were not to be that easily shifted. In despair, his father called on his solicitor, William Whitton, to help bring the boy back into line. Learning that a third party had been brought in to negotiate with him on his father's behalf, Shelley was enraged, and it took the intervention of an uncle (the kindly Captain Pinfold, Shelley's mother's brother) to broker something like a truce. A lunch was arranged on 17th April between father and son at Miller's Hotel at the eastern end of Westminster Bridge. Timothy may not have approved of the influence of his son's co-expulsee, but Hogg came along nonetheless to make up the party. 'He told me that his father would behave strangely, and that I must be prepared for him…'

Apart from the ongoing skirmishes with his father ('Father is as fierce as a lion again…'), Shelley seems to have had an agreeable, rather relaxing summer away from university. In London he visited Harriet's family the Groves, and Tom Medwin; he travelled to Cwm Elan in Wales, where Thomas Grove had a house (on a later visit to Cwm Elan he would remember this first visit in a beautiful poem, 'Retrospect') – but this was no fun, as he wrote to Hogg, quoting Hamlet: 'This is most divine scenery; but all very dull, stale, flat, and unprofitable: indeed, this place is a very great bore.'

During the summer's roaming, Hogg (with whom Shelley had been hopefully trying to set up his sister Elizabeth) had moved up to settle in York; Shelley, meanwhile, came down to spend a part of his summer back at Field Place and there made a new good friend. Elizabeth Hitchener was a schoolmistress in her late twenties, teacher to one of Captain Pilfold's daughters at Hurstpierpoint. Her intellectual curiosity and a certain revolutionary sympathy appealed to Shelley, who seems to have regarded her as a likely candidate for an ideological soulmate, and he took on the task of improving her with enthusiasm. For however long the relationship lasted, he would be a devoted teacher, a prolific correspondent and a good friend.

Thy lover, Harriet...

An even more important character enters the story here, however: Harriet Westbrook. And by the time August 1811 came to an end, Shelley would have married her.

He had met Harriet, a vintner's daughter, through his sisters – they were schoolmates at Mrs Fenning's in Clapham – and the two teenagers began a correspondence. Harriet was unhappy at school, feeling penned in there, and perhaps falling in love with Shelley too. One of her letters that reached him in Wales conveyed such distress that he hastened back to Sussex, to her; as so often with Shelley, he found himself called by some great sense of duty to do good by the world, and here was a young girl who needed saving. This, at least, was how Shelley portrayed the affair. The young couple eloped, heading north by coach towards Scotland as Harriet, at sixteen, was under age by English law. Stopping at York, where Hogg was serving his legal apprenticeship (and where he could lend them money), they arrived in Edinburgh on 28th August, and married the following day.

The register for August 28, 1811, reads 'Percy Bysshe Shelley, Farmer, Sussex, and Miss Harriet Westbrook, ... daughter of Mr John Westbrook, London.' The groom's father back home, with his wayward son so obviously absent from management of the family estates, might have flinched at that 'Farmer'.

Shelley had been ardently opposed to the institution of marriage, so his decision to wed Harriet Westbrook surprised those who knew of his free-love views – what he called, after William Godwin, the 'Godwinian plan'. He had written less than four months earlier, '… marriage, Godwin says, is hateful, detestable. A kind of ineffable, sickening disgust seizes my mind when I think of this most despotic, most unrequired fetter which prejudice has forged to confine its energies.'

Thanks to some money from good Captain Pilfold (though under express instructions from his brother-in-law not to help the wastrel youth), the newlyweds were able to honeymoon in Edinburgh, staying the whole month of September. When Hogg visited them there, at their large, rather smart place at 60 George Street, he found them happy, reading and translating, watching the passing of a great comet and contemplating the stars. 'The heavens are the home of a divine poet,' wrote Hogg; 'the stars are his nearest kindred.' Hogg obligingly approved of his friend's bride, praising her reading voice and appearance – 'bright, blooming, radiant with youth, health and beauty'. Shelley agreed, recognising his good fortune – or good judgement? – in having Harriet for a wife.

Evening: to Harriet

O thou bright Sun! beneath the dark blue line
　　Of western distance that sublime descendest,
　　And, gleaming lovelier as thy beams decline,
　　Thy million hues to every vapour lendest,
And, over cobweb lawn and grove and stream
　　Sheddest the liquid magic of thy light,
　　Till calm Earth, with the parting splendour bright,
　　Shows like the vision of a beauteous dream;
What gazer now with astronomic eye
　　Could coldly count the spots within thy sphere?
　　Such were thy lover, Harriet, could he fly
The thoughts of all that makes his passion dear.

> *And, turning senseless from thy warm caress,*
> *Pick flaws in our close-woven happiness.*

By early October the young Mr and Mrs Shelley had moved down to York, to 20 Coney Street on the bank of the Ouse; and later in October Shelley travelled down to Cuckfield in Sussex to meet his uncle in the hope of securing some reasonable financial terms with his father. 'I am now with my uncle,' he wrote; 'he is a hearty fellow, and has behaved very nobly to me, in return for which I have illuminated him.'

During Shelley's absence, his friend Hogg would look after his young bride. But Shelley and Hogg had long argued in favour of communal property and against the exclusivity of marriage, and in this spirit of sharing Hogg sought (in his friend's absence) to wrangle his fair share of Harriet. Harriet herself was no adherent of the Godwinian plan, and Shelley returned to York to find his wife distraught at Hogg's advances; she persuaded him to leave York and his friend at once, and head west.

In the correspondence that followed with the desperate Hogg, it seems that – far from being angry – Shelley is acting only in his friend's interest. 'I do not know that absence will *certainly* cure love...' he writes to York in November. But in his letters to Elizabeth Hitchener his anger at his friend's betrayal is not hidden: 'You know I came to Sussex to settle my affairs, and left Harriet at York under the protection of Hogg. You know the implicit faith I had in him, the unalterableness of my attachment, the exalted thoughts I entertained of his excellence. Can you then conceive that he would have attempted to *seduce my wife*?' And later, 'Hogg at length has declared himself to be one of those mad votaries of selfishness who are cool to destroy the peace of others, and revengeful when their schemes are destroyed, even to idiotism...'

So Shelley and Harriet set off for Keswick (in what is now Cumbria), with Harriet's sister Eliza in tow. (Eliza did not like

Shelley, incidentally, nor he her – and they would trouble each other's lives significantly for many years yet.) At Keswick they settled at Chestnut Cottage, Chestnut Hill, on the Penrith Road, and Shelley took advantage of their proximity to seek out the company of one of the men he most admired in the world, the poet Robert Southey.

Robert Southey – now an elderly thirty-seven – had been acclaimed as the author of, among other things, numerous ballads and translations, and *Madoc*, an epic narrative poem. He was respected, regularly published and widely read. Just a couple of years later, on the death of Henry James Pye, he would be named the new Poet Laureate (though admittedly only after Walter Scott had turned it down), a post he would occupy until his death in 1843. Shelley's favourite of Southey's works was his Arabian verse romance *Thalaba*; but he admired his politics too – Southey was a man with radical views on liberty, who seventeen years earlier had planned with Coleridge to establish a utopian community in New England.

Shelley and Southey had a friend in common, William Calvert, at whose home the younger man was introduced to his idol. The older poet received him kindly, but the meeting was not all Shelley had hoped for. He found Southey disappointing, nothing the youthful and radical hero he had expected:

'Southey has changed. I shall see him soon, and I shall reproach him for his tergiversation. – He to whom Bigotry, Tyranny, Law was hateful, has become the votary of these idols in a form the most disgusting.'

The Shelleys (and sister-in-law Eliza) spent most of the winter at Keswick. Shelley wrote a considerable amount during his time here, not only some poetry and political pamphletry but also correspondence, in particular to his Sussex friend Elizabeth Hitchener. In early December they visited the Duke of Norfolk (Timothy Shelley's old ally) at his castle, Greystoke, not far from Keswick, where the old man made another attempt to broker a peace between father and son, this time with some limited success.

After the disappointment with Southey, it must have been with some trepidation that Shelley assailed another of his idols, the atheist philosopher William Godwin, to whom he wrote for the first time in early January 1812.

Thanks to the encouraging Dr Lind, Shelley had read Godwin's *Enquiry Concerning Political Justice* while still at Eton, and had come to revere the man who epitomised for him rationalism and a belief in the perfectibility of mankind (the possibility, that is, for continuous and infinite improvement to the human race and human society). Shelley would believe the same, and would spend much of his life, one way or another, striving for this improvement. He was, one might say, a social optimist, keen on the advancement of knowledge and passionate about the possibility of progress, and born with a sense of his own destiny to help effect that positive change. One of the main rallying points of this struggle was the fight against tyranny – indeed, any form of authority, of which monarchy was seen as a particularly egregious example.

His first letter to Godwin described Shelley's enthusiasm for the old philosopher (while also saying, essentially, 'You know, I thought you were dead, actually…'):

The name of Godwin has been used to excite in me feelings of reverence and admiration. I have been accustomed to consider him a luminary too dazzling for the darkness which surrounds him. From the earliest period of my knowledge of his principles, I have ardently desired to share, on the footing of intimacy, that intellect which I have delighted to contemplate in its emanations.

This gushing letter elicited a response from the older man within a few days. Godwin pointed out in his reply that Shelley's first missive had revealed so little of himself, so on the 10th of the month Shelley produced to order another very long, more autobiographical letter:

I am the son of a man of fortune in Sussex. The habits of thinking of my father and myself never coincided... I was haunted with a passion for the wildest and most extra-vagant romances... went to Oxford... Classical reading and poetical writing... printed a pamphlet... was expelled... led me to regard the law of primogeniture an evil of primary magnitude...

... and on and on he goes.

(Godwin would later sum up what he had learned of Shelley most succinctly: 'Your family consists of yourself, a very young wife, and a sister. Yourself, as I conceive, a plain philosophical republican, loving your species very much, and caring little for the accumulation of personal indulgences – Tell me, how much truth is there in this picture?')

On 19th January the Shelleys' calm lakeside lives were rocked by a midnight break-in to Chestnut Cottage, the motives for which remain confused. Shelley was especially shaken, but decided to characterise it as nothing more sinister than a random attempted robbery, dismissing 'all fears of assassins, and spies and prisons'. Still, everyone felt rather less comfortable in their safe little home now.

Meanwhile in Ireland, just over the water from Keswick, there were political troubles brewing. Sectarian unrest had followed the signing of the Act of Union in 1801 (which merged the United Kingdom and Ireland into a single kingdom), and even now, over a decade later, the promised emancipation of the Catholics had yet to materialise.

The Catholic cause, and the cause of Peace and Tolerance in the more abstract, clearly needed help, so off Shelley went. It was early February 1812 when they left cold Keswick, and a disapproving Robert Southey, behind them. (Shelley was always eliciting the disapproval of his elders, though, so this was hardly a novelty.) Hogg too thought the whole trip a silly whim: 'I had never heard him mention Catholic Emancipation, or Catholic

Disabilities; and I do not believe that he ever had any definite notion of the meaning of these party phrases...'

Elizabeth Hitchener refused an invitation to join the party, in spite of much importuning from Shelley; so it was just Shelley, his wife and his sister-in-law, setting off on their private campaign, with a great deal of political fervour and very little money. (Shelley figured that *in extremis* he could always raise a little money by publishing some poems while he was out there – suggesting a rather different market for poetry to today's...)

It was never going to be easy, and there were risks, as Shelley well knew. 'Shall I not get into prison? Harriet is sadly afraid that his Majesty will provide me with a lodging, in consideration of the zeal which I evince for the bettering of his subjects.' But Shelley was never less than ambitious, and never less than optimistic for the possibility of good progress.

They crossed the water roughly by storm-blown boat, then a land journey took them to Dublin, where they lodged above a draper's at 7 Sackville Street. Shelley's recent writing had included a pamphlet, *Address to the Irish People*, which he had printed and in the first fortnight distributed some 400 copies. Some of these were distributed in pubs, others by Shelley standing at his window and throwing copies at any passer-by 'who looked likely'. The pamphlet, pro-emancipation and encouraging self-improvement as a way towards enlightened tolerance, did not make Shelley particularly popular with either side.

Dublin, for Shelley, was not the easiest place to be. 'I had no conception of the depth of human misery until now,' he wrote to Godwin. 'The poor of Dublin are assuredly the meanest and most miserable of all. In their narrow streets thousands seem huddled together – one mass of animated filth. With what eagerness do such scenes as these inspire me!' Two days later he was writing to Elizabeth Hitchener: 'I am sick of this city, and long to be with you and peace. The rich *grind* the poor into abjectness, and then complain that they are abject. They goad them to famine, and hang them if they steal a loaf. – Well, adieu to this!'

The Shelleys did at least make one good friend in Dublin, the republican spinster Catherine Nugent, a fine character described by Blunden as 'one of those women whose reward is in heaven'. She would support the Shelleys in their work, and her friendship with Harriet would be sustained in letters until Harriet's death.

While in Ireland Shelley took the opportunity to espouse another cause too, the dismantling of the 1801 union itself. He published the snappily titled *Proposals for an Association of Philanthropists who convinced of the inadequacy of the moral and political state of Ireland to produce benefits which are nevertheless attainable are willing to unite to accomplish its regeneration*. This time it was Godwin who disapproved (at a distance), and who sought (with some success) to convince Shelley to abandon his ideas of quick, sharp, sudden change in favour of taking a longer, more pacific view.

A broadsheet *Declaration of Rights* was yet another publication to come out of Shelley's Irish visit – many copies of this were sent to Elizabeth Hitchener in the hope that she might coordinate Sussex distribution.

Having expanded his party to include the addition of man-servant Daniel Healy, Shelley left Dublin on 4th April. Healy had been employed by the Shelleys in Dublin to help distribute pamphlets; sadly he may also have been, as Richard Holmes points out, 'their only Irish convert'.

Having failed to identify somewhere to live in Sussex, and deciding against joining Elizabeth Hitchener at Hurstpierpoint, the Shelleys and their household made instead south-eastwards from Holyhead, crossing down through Wales till they stopped at Nantgwillt, a big old farmhouse in Radnorshire. This turned out to be only a temporary solution – to the disappointment of Shelley, who liked the place and hoped to have been able to stay – and they returned briefly to the Groves' house at Cwm Elan nearby. Next, on to Devon...

Late June saw the Shelleys and their entourage settled at Lynmouth in north Devon; they had been passing through on their way to Ilfracombe and fallen in love with the fishing village and the cottage they found there. Shelley wrote to Godwin:

> This place is beautiful; it equals – Harriet says it exceeds – Nantgwillt. Mountains certainly of not less perpendicular elevation than 1,000 feet are broken abruptly into valleys of indescribable fertility and grandeur. The climate is so mild, that myrtles of an immense size twine up our cottage, and roses blow in the open air in winter. In addition to these is the sea, which dashes against a rocky and caverned shore, presenting an ever-changing view. All 'shows of sky and earth, of sea and valley' are here.

(Hogg commented rather acidly, 'It is only up the imagination of a poet, that the myrtle ever twines.')

The party were joined now by Elizabeth Hitchener, for a domestic arrangement which raised some eyebrows back in Sussex; her reputation would never be quite the same again...

At Lynmouth Shelley continued to write pieces of political trouble, some of which he distributed by releasing them in bottles into the Bristol Channel. Some copies of the *Declaration* were dispatched aloft across the Channel carried by little hot-air balloons of the Shelleys' own making.

To a Balloon, Laden with Knowledge

Bright ball of flame that through the gloom of even
  Silently takest thine aethereal way,
  And with surpassing glory dimm'st each ray
Twinkling amid the dark blue depths of Heaven, –
Unlike the Fire thou bearest, soon shall thou
  Fade like a meteor in surrounding gloom,

Whilst that, unquencheable, is doomed to glow
    A watch-light by the patriot's lonely tomb;
A ray of courage to the oppressed and poor,
    A spark, though gleaming on the hovel's hearth,
Which through the tyrant's gilded domes shall roar;
    A beacon in the darkness of the Earth;
A Sun which o'er the renovated scene
Shall dart like Truth where Falsehood yet has been.

He wrote 'Letter to Lord Ellenborough' here at Lynmouth, too, and this particular bit of provocation got Daniel Healy briefly arrested – Shelley had in fact been trying to get rid of him, but presumably hadn't quite intended this – and Shelley was placed under the observation of certain agencies of state security. Unsurprisingly, it was not the first time his name had been brought to their attention…

Not the veriest slave that e'er crawled on the loathing earth...

The closing months of 1812 uprooted the Shelleys yet again, this time to Tremadoc, an idealist society planned and built by William Maddocks – a man of a rare breed: a pioneering, idealist MP – close to the west coast of north Wales. The planned central area of Tremadoc had just been completed when Shelley heard of the scheme, and moved down to live there, and to lend a hand.

There was a mansion at Tremadoc – Tan-yr-allt – which was standing empty, so Maddocks invited Shelley to move in, and Shelley began to work for him on the management of the great project, and in trying to raise funds to develop it. Hogg visited him here (their friendship now restored after that unfortunate little attempted wife-sharing episode), and commented on Shelley's adoption of the Tremadoc plans 'after his manner, and with a zeal far too hot to hold'. The Shelleys were able to spend some time with Godwin too, having first met the philosopher in person in October.

In November Elizabeth Hitchener left the party; Shelley had come to tire of the attractions of her mind, and Harriet was none too keen on this older woman seducing her husband with any other charms. She returned to teaching and seems not to have been much missed from the household – though once much loved by Shelley, he had come by now to refer to his 'later tormentor and schoolmistress' as the 'Brown Demon'.

Apparently, she had shown herself to be an 'artful, superficial, ugly, hermaphroditical beast of a woman, and my astonishment at my fatuity, inconsistency, and bad taste was never so great, as after living four months with her as an inmate'.

And then there was the poetry. For all his managerial work for Maddocks at Tremadoc, for all the social interaction and the day-to-day of domestic life, Shelley found time to work on what would be his first major piece of poetic work, *Queen Mab*.

Queen Mab – in the finished form by which we know it today – is an incredibly assured piece of work for such a young, relatively inexperienced writer. It begins with the Fairy Queen waking a woman – Ianthe – and taking her in her chariot on a journey of great visions; and then goes on to a determined attack on what would come to be Shelley's regular targets: monarchy, religion, and so on. Instead of these evils it preaches atheism, republicanism, and free love in place of marriage. The arguments in the poem are sustained in more than a dozen mini-essay notes that accompany it, including 'There is no God' and 'Even love is sold'. The notes and the poem combine to make a powerful (if sometimes chaotic) statement of the poet's political views, as, for example, in this passage, from part four:

> 'Then grave and hoary-headed hypocrites,
> Without a hope, a passion or a love,
> Who, through a life of luxury and lies
> Have crept by flattery to the seats of power,
> Support the system whence their honours flow…
> They have three words: – well tyrants know their use,
> Well pay them for the loan, with usury
> Torn from a bleeding world! – God, Hell and Heaven.
> A vengeful, pitiless, and almighty fiend,
> Whose mercy is a nickname for the rage
> Of tameless tigers hungering for blood.
> Hell, a red gulf of everlasting fire,
> Where poisonous and undying worms prolong

Eternal misery to those hapless slaves
Whose life has been a penance for its crimes.
And Heaven, a meed for those who dare belie
Their human nature, quake, believe, and cringe
Before the mockeries of earthly power.

'These tools the tyrant tempers to his work,
Wields in his wrath, and as he wills destroys,
Omnipotent in wickedness: the while
Youth springs, age moulders, manhood tamely does
His bidding, bribed by short-lived joys to lend
Force to the weakness of his trembling arm.
They rise, they fall; one generation comes
Yielding its harvest to destruction's scythe.
It fades, another blossoms; yet behold!
Red glows the tyrant's stamp-mark on its bloom,
Withering and cankering deep its passive prime.
He has invented lying words and modes,
Empty and vain as his own coreless heart;
Evasive meanings, nothings of much sound,
To lure the heedless victim to the toils
Spread round the valley of its paradise.

'Look to thyself, priest, conqueror, or prince!
Whether thy trade is falsehood, and thy lusts
Deep wallow in the earnings of the poor,
With whom thy master was: – or thou delight'st
In numbering o'er the myriads of thy slain,
All misery weighing nothing in the scale
Against thy short-lived fame; or thou dost load
With cowardice and crime the groaning land,
A pomp-fed king. Look to thy wretched self!
Ay, art thou not the veriest slave that e'er
Crawled on the loathing earth? Are not thy days
Days of unsatisfying listlessness?

Dost thou not cry, ere night's long rack is o'er,
"When will the morning come?" Is not thy youth
A vain and feverish dream of sensualism?
Thy manhood blighted with unripe disease?
Are not thy views of unregretted death
Drear, comfortless, and horrible? Thy mind,
Is it not morbid as thy nerveless frame,
Incapable of judgement, hope or love?
And dost thou wish the errors to survive,
That bar thee from all sympathies of good,
After the miserable interest
Thou hold'st in their protraction? When the grave
Has swallowed up thy memory and thyself,
Dost thou desire the bane that poisons earth
To twine its roots around thy coffined clay,
Spring from thy bones, and blossom on thy tomb,
That of its fruit thy babes may eat and die?

One of the many particular messages of *Queen Mab* is the benefit of a vegetarian life – 'the Pythagorean system', Shelley called it. He and Harriet were both vegetarians, though the return journey from Dublin had seen a slight lapse... That moment of weakness notwithstanding, Shelley was becoming an increasingly devoted follower of vegetarianism guru J.P. Newton, and would himself write pieces in support of the movement, including the pamphlet *On the Vegetable System of Diet*.

Tremadoc, which had promised so much, was not, however, an unmitigated success. 'The society in Wales is very stupid. They are all aristocrats and saints...' And then there was the weather: 'The thermometer is twelve degrees below freezing; this is Russian cold!' Shelley wrote in January.

The Shelleys' months at Tremadoc came to an odd end in February 1813, with an incident that has still not been explained satisfactorily. Late in the night of the 26th Shelley came downstairs with a loaded pistol, and shots were fired. Had there been an intruder? Was the assailant (as was suggested at one time) a farmer taking revenge for some sheep of his lately shot by the young poet? Was this the work of local people who didn't approve of these outsiders colonising their land? Or was the whole thing a figment of Shelley's always lively imagination?

Shelley wrote an unusually short (but typically excitable) letter to Thomas Hookham, a printer of his acquaintance on Old Bond Street: 'Dear Sir, I have just escaped an atrocious assassination. Oh, send £20 if you have it! You will perhaps hear of me no more! Your friend, Percy Shelley.'

Whatever the explanation for the nocturnal drama, Shelley, Harriet and Eliza were out before the month was over, and on their way back to Dublin. From Dublin, Shelley sent the great manuscript of *Queen Mab* down to Hookham in London: 'I shall expect no success, Let only 250 copies be printed – a small neat quarto, on fine paper, and so as to catch the aristocrats. They will not read it, but their sons and daughters may…'

That done, the family travelled south-west to Killarney, taking a cottage on one of the lake islands for a holiday. The weather was rough and disagreeable, however, and the holiday was not to last long. Soon enough, a letter arrived from Hogg, and Shelley was back on the move – back to Dublin, to meet up with his old friend, and then to London.

I love thee, Baby!
for thine own sweet sake…

Shelley was in poor health these days – indeed, for much of the rest of his life he would be afflicted with a shifting combination of consumption, abdominal pains, ophthalmia and other ailments – and Hogg wrote to Harriet, 'I am very sorry that Bysshe is unwell. It is hard that his heart should be so good, and his head so bad: I wish you had as much influence over the latter as over the former.'

The London season was an unsettled time for the Shelleys, moving as they did between Grove House at 23 Chapel Street in Grosvenor Square (home to Harriet's parents, and the address that would be given on the title page of *Queen Mab* when it appeared in May), rooms at Cooke's Hotel (on Albemarle Street, off Piccadilly) and rooms at Half Moon Street just down the road. Here, wrote Hogg, 'There was a little projecting window… in which Shelley might be seen from the street all day long, book in hand, with lively gestures and bright eyes; so that Mrs. N. said, he wanted only a pan of clear water and a fresh turf to look like some young lady's lark, hanging outside for air and song.' Hogg would also remember Half Moon Street for the quality of the food he was served there:

Some considerable time after the appointed hour, a roasted shoulder of mutton, of the coarsest, toughest grain, graced, or disgraced, the ill-supplied table; the watery gravy that issued from the perverse joint, when it was cut, a duty commonly assigned to me, seemed the most apt of all things to embody the conception of penury and utter destitution. There were potatoes in every respect worthy of the mutton; and the cheese, which was either forgotten or uneatable, closed the ungenial repast...

It was at Cooke's that Shelley was resident when called on by the Duke of Norfolk for the latest attempt to resolve differences with his father; the most insurmountable obstacle to the resolution of these differences was Timothy's predictable insistence on his son's return to the Christian fold, and Shelley's own equally predictable refusal to do anything of the sort.

In June of 1813, Harriet gave birth to the couple's first child; she was given a name from *Queen Mab*:

To Ianthe

I love thee, Baby! for thine own sweet sake;
    Those azure eyes, that faintly dimpled cheek,
    Thy tender frame, so eloquently weak,
    Love in the sternest heart of hate might wake;
But more when o'er thy fitful slumber bending
    Thy mother folds thee to her wakeful heart,
    Whilst love and pity, in her glances blending,
    All that thy passive eyes can feel impart:
More, when some feeble lineaments of her,
    Who bore thy weight beneath her spotless bosom,
    As with deep love I read thy face, recur, –
More dear art thou, O fair and fragile blossom;
    Dearest when most thy tender traits express
    The image of thy mother's loveliness.

The couple and their baby girl moved to Bracknell, near Windsor. With his writing flowing easily, with the new baby and the move to a new home, things promised well.

And indeed Shelley did find much to cherish in this new phase of his life. Most importantly, Bracknell provided him with some significant and lasting new friendships. There was the lately widowed Madame de Boinville (sister-in-law to the vegetarian Newton), with her daughter Cornelia, who lived at High Elms House and in whose house the Shelleys stayed; the de Boinvilles' was a home filled with lively political and intellectual discussion, and which frequently kept Shelley away from his own family (attracted perhaps to Cornelia too, lately married though she was...). And in some respects most interestingly for our purposes, there was the kindling now of a new friendship with the satirist and poet Thomas Love Peacock, resident at Marlow nearby, who would capture Shelley memorably in his own writing a few years later.

Looking outside his little domestic circle, we find Shelley's infamy increasing. Hookham (through whom, in fact, Shelley and Peacock had met) had said he would not publish *Queen Mab*, so the poem's author had printed it and distributed many copies of it himself, and on the whole it was not favourably received. Indeed, with this work so consistently popular among radicals and radical publishers, bootleg editions for years and years afterwards would cause him all kinds of trouble. So – with this work just two months old – Shelley's respectability was hardly at its height when he decided, in late July, to return to Field Place to visit his mother, his father being conveniently away from home. He arrived – disguised! – around the date of his twenty-first birthday, for what would be his final visit to Field Place. This landmark birthday (and certain pressing demands for payment) meant that the resolution of questions of inheritance money was more urgent than ever.

It is interesting to remember here what Shelley had written in his first letter to Leigh Hunt (who would become a close friend) some years before this: 'My father is in parliament, and on attaining twenty-one, I shall in all probability fill his seat...' By now – turning twenty-one at last – it would have been hard to remember that there was once a time when Shelley had had faith in this proposed career path.

By autumn 1813 the Shelleys were – again – looking for a permanent home. They went first to Ambleside in the Lake District, then on to Edinburgh, and finally back down to a home Shelley had found for them close to Windsor. By the end of the year the couple, baby Ianthe and her aunt Eliza were living here, at Easthampstead. This was Shelley's second return to the area of his Eton schooldays, and it reunited him, after only a brief absence, with those nearby neighbourhood friends of his, Peacock at Marlow and the de Boinvilles at Bracknell.

Again, the de Boinvilles would open their home to Shelley, sometimes for extended periods, as his marriage became increasingly cool. One visit spanned late February and early March, and he only finally left because he needed to travel to London, rather than because he felt any sense of duty to return to his own domestic setting. His errand this time was to arrange a legal shoring-up of his marriage to Harriet, to regularise their first (Scottish) marriage with a ceremony in the English Church, in the hope that this would help to resolve any doubts about his children's rights to the family inheritance. (A wise move, as even under Scottish law the legitimacy of their first marriage was questionable.) Harriet joined him in London and they were (re-)married on 24th March, at St George's Church, Hanover Square, and together returned home. By the middle of the following month Shelley was back with the de Boinvilles and Harriet with Eliza at Bath. But the re-marriage of convenience had brought at least a brief spell of détente. By the start of April, Shelley and Harriet were expecting their second child.

After the marriage ceremony Harriet kept away from London for a time. The city had its hazards, not least the questionably healthy lure of the Godwin household on Skinner Street. For one thing, Harriet didn't like Mrs Godwin at all; but this would soon be the least of her troubles, for when Shelley visited the old philosopher in June he found Godwin's daughter Mary there too (Shelley had seen her once or twice before, but only ever briefly) – and the moment that Shelley and Mary met, Harriet's marriage was all but over.

My sweetest friend...

Shelley would be described by the painter Joseph Severn as having:

> ... a countenance painfully intellectual, inasmuch as it showed traces of his struggle with humanity, and betrayed the abstract gift of a high mind in little relation with the world. His restless blue eye appeared to dwell more on the inward than the outward aspect of nature. His manner, aristocratic though gentle, aided his personal beauty. Fine classical features, luxuriant brown hair, and a slightly ruddy complexion, combined with his unconsciousness of his attractive appearance, added to his fine exterior.

He was slender, tall (or at least, said Horace Smith, 'would have been tall had he carried himself upright'), with delicate features, bright eyes, a high-pitched voice, a manner somehow shy but also fierily passionate. And this was the man with whom young Mary would fall in love in an instant.

Mary Shelley, née Godwin, was Godwin's daughter by Mary Wollstonecraft, the author of the landmark work of feminist philosophy *A Vindication of the Rights of Woman*, who had died of septicaemia following Mary's birth. When she met Shelley in 1814, Mary had just returned to London from a few months spent in Dundee; at sixteen, she was about to escape at last from her years of educational discipline, while he was unhappy in a marriage which had not been born out of any great love – or not on his part, at least. Just days after meeting they were together at St Pancras cemetery, paying respects to the grave of Mary's mother, and here they declared their love for each other.

The pregnant Harriet had moved to Bath, but Shelley invited her back to London, took her with him to see Godwin, and told her about Mary. She fell instantly ill.

In many ways Harriet had been a promising young wife to Shelley – intelligent, attractive, supportive, ready to follow him devotedly, getting suitably enthusiastic about his work and passions. But the relationship was no longer what it had been, with conflicts about her ever-present sister Eliza, and about his relationship (or not) with Mme de Boinville's delightful daughter Cornelia, about the influence of the Godwins and more; for his part the appeal of rescuing and educating her (as he had done Elizabeth Hitchener) had waned, and he seems to have felt no emotional dependency on her, however she may still have felt about him. Her time was over. And just as he had done with Harriet three years before, on 28th July Shelley eloped with young Mary Godwin. She was (just as Harriet had been on that first elopement) still only sixteen, Shelley not quite twenty-two.

Early on that morning Mary and her stepsister Jane Clairmont left Skinner Street and made their way to Hatton Garden, where Shelley was waiting for them; the trio set off down to Dover. (The second Mrs Godwin – Jane's mother – hoped to change her daughter's mind, and followed the escapees down as far as Calais, but with no luck.) Then a hasty journey across France – a country newly at peace after years of turmoil and war, by this point almost concluded with Napoleon's abdication and exile to Elba in the May just past – to Paris, to Troyes (where an irrepressibly optimistic Shelley wrote to Harriet to ask her if she might like to join them?), walking and riding, reading and writing as they went (Shelley was working on his novella *The Assassins*, which was never completed); then to Neuchâtel and Brunnen in Switzerland, where finally they took rooms on Lake Lucerne.

Feelings of a Republican on
the Fall of Bonaparte

I hated thee, fallen tyrant! I did groan
To think that a most unambitious slave,
Like thou, shouldst dance and revel on the grave
Of Liberty. Thou mightst have built thy throne
Where it had stood even now: thou didst prefer
A frail and bloody pomp which Time has swept
In fragments towards Oblivion. Massacre,
For this I prayed, would on thy sleep have crept,
Treason and Slavery, Rapine, Fear, and Lust,
And stifled thee, their minister. I know
Too late, since thou and France are in the dust,
That Virtue owns a more eternal foe
Than Force or Fraud: old Custom, legal Crime,
And bloody Faith the foulest birth of Time.

Shelley and his companions didn't stay long – the money in the coffers soon ran out, somewhat predictably – and before long were heading back home. They travelled by water, first, down the Reuss and Rhine to Bonn, then overland to Rotterdam, and by boat again to Gravesend. This last leg had to be taken on an IOU to the ship's captain, a credit note that it fell to Harriet to settle.

Shelley was being pursued by bailiffs now. But his money troubles were not all of his own making, and were certainly not due to his own unusual profligacy – among the greatest drains on his purse was his distinguished new father-in-law, William Godwin, who had been claiming money from him with irritating frequency. Though Godwin claims to have felt betrayed by the young poet who, as he saw it, seduced his daughter and stole her away, he had no problem expecting that poet to bankroll him to a sometimes extraordinary degree.

By 13th September the high-speed European elopement tour had come to an end, and Shelley and Mary (and Jane) were back in London. Another of those periods of rather nomadic life in the capital would follow – a fortnight at 56 Margaret Street, Cavendish Square; then 5 Church Terrace behind St Pancras (not far from the spot where the couple had first declared their love to each other); the Cross Keys Inn on St John's Street; and 2 Nelson Square, off the Blackfriars Road. Hogg was back in the picture now, and again obligingly approved of his friend's choice of partner. And again sought to seduce her for himself. (With no more success than he had found with Harriet, unsurprisingly.)

Back at the Westbrooks' on Chapel Street, meanwhile, Shelley's second child was born to Harriet, about a month prematurely, on 30th November – Charles Bysshe Shelley. It was a week before Shelley learned the news.

Young Charles's namesake, old Sir Bysshe Shelley, died in the first week of January, aged eighty-three, his baronetcy passing down to Timothy. For Shelley, who had little love to spare for his grandfather, the old man's death was taken as rather good news, releasing as it did a significant inheritance. 'He is a bad man,' Shelley had written a few years earlier. 'I never had respect for him: I always regarded him as a curse on society. I shall not grieve at his death. I will not wear mourning: I will not attend his funeral.'

Shelley and Claire Clairmont (Mary's stepsister Jane had now decided to be known as Claire) came down to Sussex for the reading of the old man's will, though they were denied access and Shelley sat outside, on the Field Place doorstep, reading his Milton, to await the verdict.

The promise of money that the will would bring allowed Shelley to take a large apartment in London, at Hans Place, near

Knightsbridge. Here, in late February, Mary would give birth prematurely to a child, but the baby died a fortnight later.

I

They die – the dead return not – Misery
  Sits near an open grave and calls them over,
A Youth with hoary hair and haggard eye –
  They are the names of kindred, friend and lover,
Which he so feebly calls – they all are gone –
Fond wretch, all dead! those vacant names alone,
  This most familiar scene, my pain –
  These tombs – alone remain.

II

Misery, my sweetest friend – oh, weep no more!
  Thou wilt not be consoled – I wonder not!
For I have seen thee from thy dwelling's door
  Watch the calm sunset with them, and this spot
Was even as bright and calm, but transitory,
And now thy hopes are gone, thy hair is hoary;
  This most familiar scene, my pain –
  These tombs – alone remain.

Shelley too was ailing at this time. And still the gruelling London odyssey continued; Arabella Road in Pimlico was next, and then to Bloomsbury, 26 Marchmont Street.

May 1815 saw a real, robust financial agreement reached between Timothy Shelley and his son, at long last: a thousand pounds a year. The following month Shelley and Mary holidayed in Torquay, Claire having detached herself from the household for a few months. Then, with Mary (now pregnant again) waiting in Clifton, Shelley returned to his usual Windsor environs to find the family a home; they took a cottage at Bishopsgate, beside Windsor Park.

The time the Shelleys spent at Bishopsgate was a happy one. They were visited often by friends such as Peacock, still living nearby at Marlow, and the rehabilitated Hogg; they talked for hours ('I have often wished,' wrote Hogg, '– vainly wished – that one at least of the twelve shorthand writers had been placed behind a screen during Bysshe's nightly colloquies, to catch and secure for ever on paper a philosophical apocalypse, of which the duration was unhappily so transient'), they read aloud; they walked, and took boats out on the river. One such trip, in August, took Shelley, Mary, Peacock and Claire's brother Charles Clairmont upriver through Oxford (where Shelley's stalwart vegetarianism lapsed over some mutton chops) to just beyond Lechlade in Gloucestershire.

A Summer Evening Churchyard
Lechlade, Gloucestershire

The wind has swept from the wide atmosphere
Each vapour that obscured the sunset's ray;
And pallid Evening twines its beaming hair
In duskier braids around the languid eyes of Day:
Silence and Twilight, unbeloved of men,
Creep hand in hand from yon obscurest glen.

They breathe their spells towards the departing day,
Encompassing the earth, air, stars, and sea;
Light, sound, and motion own the potent sway,
Responding to the charm with its own mystery.
The winds are still, or the dry church-tower grass
Knows not their gentle motions as they pass.

Thou too, aërial Pile! whose pinnacles
Point from one shrine like pyramids of fire,
Obeyest in silence their sweet solemn spells,

Clothing in hues of heaven thy dim and distant spire,
Around whose lessening and invisible height
Gather among the stars the clouds of night.

The dead are sleeping in their sepulchres:
And, mouldering as they sleep, a thrilling sound,
Half sense, half thought, among the darkness stirs,
Breathed from their wormy beds all living things around,
And, mingling with the still night and mute sky,
Its awful hush is felt inaudibly.

Thus solemnized and softened, death is mild
And terrorless as this serenest night:
Here could I hope, like some enquiring child
Sporting on graves, that death did hide from human sight
Sweet secrets, or beside its breathless sleep
That loveliest dreams perpetual watch did keep.

The excursion would inspire another poem, too, and a significant one in the canon of early Shelley work. *Alastor, or the Spirit of Solitude*, is a non-political poem, a piece of blank-verse narrative, in which a poet (perhaps based on Wordsworth) tries to escape beyond the natural world to the supernatural; he sees a vision of a supernatural world and a dream-maiden...

Shelley completed the preface to *Alastor* on 14th December 1815, and the poem was published the following February. In the intervening month, Mary had given birth at Bishopsgate to a baby boy, whom they christened William.

Mont Blanc yet gleams on high…

The spring of 1816 saw the Shelleys in London again, again moving between a variety of addresses (including a return to Marchmont Street), and again cohabiting with Claire Clairmont. She had taken on a role which Shelley and his marriages seemed to invite, of the intimately cohabiting third party – a mantle worn previously by both Eliza Westbrook and Elizabeth Hitchener.

They did not stay long in the capital, though, as Europe was calling them back; calling Claire in particular, in the person of the recently departed Lord Byron, who had lately been her lover. (Of this small detail Mary may not have been fully aware.)

So Shelley, Mary, baby William and Claire set off for Europe on 3rd May. By the 8th they were in Paris, and on the 10th they left for Geneva, where they arrived three days later. They took rooms at the Hotel de l'Angleterre at Sécheron, and before long Byron turned up at that very same hotel…

Home for the summer would be the Maison Chappuis, a little chalet at Montalègre, by the shores of Lake Geneva near Cologny; Byron would be just up the hill at the grander Villa Diodati (where Milton had once stayed), with the small coterie he had travelling with him. The two parties would meet up at the Diodati, where, late at night, by candlelight, Byron, Shelley and their companions would talk about poetry (Shelley was force-feeding his ungrateful friend with large doses of Wordsworth), share thoughts about the supernatural and tell each other ghost stories. One such stormy evening was the birth of one of the most famous of all supernatural tales, when a writing contest between the guests set Mary on the path to creating the book that was to make her name immortal. It was suggested that each guest would attempt to write a ghost story, and from Mary's efforts *Frankenstein* was born.

On 23rd June the two poets, Shelley and Byron, went on a sailing trip, Shelley already being a keen sailor; their trip took them around Lake Geneva, to Évian, the Château de Chillon and Lausanne, with Shelley reading Rousseau as they went ('Reading [The *Nouvelle Heloïse*] on the very spot where the scenes are laid added to the interest,' Mary wrote later) and planning a new work, which would be his *Hymn to Intellectual Beauty*. Shelley was fortunate to survive to write it, for on their return trip a squall took the boat, and Shelley did not know how to swim...

They were back on the 2nd, and later that month they were off on another excursion, this time to Chamonix. Richard Holmes has pointed out that while it was quite common for English travellers to Europe to see glorious Mont Blanc and be struck with a revelation about the existence of a magnificent divine Creator, for the devout atheist Shelley it had quite the opposite effect. It was surely clear evidence that there is no such Being. His poem 'Mont Blanc' considers great creative and destructive powers, but in a natural world that is distinctly godless.

Mont Blanc
(Lines written in the Vale of Chamouni)

I

The everlasting universe of things
Flows through the mind, and rolls its rapid waves,
Now dark – now glittering – now reflecting gloom –

Now lending splendour, where from secret springs
The source of human thought its tribute brings
Of waters, – with a sound but half its own,
Such as a feeble brook will oft assume
In the wild woods, among the mountains lone,
Where waterfalls around it leap for ever,
Where woods and winds contend, and a vast river
Over its rocks ceaselessly bursts and raves.

II

Thus thou, Ravine of Arve – dark, deep Ravine –
Thou many-coloured, many-voicèd vale,
Over whose pines, and crags, and caverns sail
Fast cloud-shadows and sunbeams: awful scene,
Where Power in likeness of the Arve comes down
From the ice-gulfs that gird his secret throne,
Bursting through these dark mountains like the flame
Of lightning through the tempest; – thou dost lie,
Thy giant brood of pines around thee clinging,
Children of elder time, in whose devotion
The chainless winds still come and ever came
To drink their odours, and their mighty swinging
To hear – an old and solemn harmony;
Thine earthly rainbows stretched across the sweep
Of the aethereal waterfall, whose veil
Robes some unsculptured image; the strange sleep
Which when the voices of the desert fail
Wraps all in its own deep eternity; –
Thy caverns echoing to the Arve's commotion,
A loud, lone sound no other sound can tame;
Thou art pervaded with that ceaseless motion,
Thou art the path of that unresting sound –
Dizzy Ravine! and when I gaze on thee
I seem as in a trance sublime and strange

To muse on my own separate fantasy,
My own, my human mind, which passively
Now renders and receives fast influencings,
Holding an unremitting interchange
With the clear universe of things around;
One legion of wild thoughts, whose wandering wings
Now float above thy darkness, and now rest
Where that or thou art no unbidden guest,
In the still cave of the witch Poesy,
Seeking among the shadows that pass by
Ghosts of all things that are, some shade of thee,
Some phantom, some faint image; till the breast
From which they fled recalls them, thou art there!

III

Some say that gleams of a remoter world
Visit the soul in sleep, – that death is slumber,
And that its shapes the busy thoughts outnumber
Of those who wake and live. – I look on high;
Has some unknown omnipotence unfurled
The veil of life and death? or do I lie
In dream, and does the mightier world of sleep
Spread far and round and inaccessibly
Its circles? For the very spirit fails,
Driven like a homeless cloud from steep to steep
That vanishes among the viewless gales!
Far, far above, piercing the infinite sky,
Mont Blanc appears, – still snowy, and serene –
Its subject mountains their unearthly forms
Pile around it, ice and rock; broad vales between
Of frozen floods, unfathomable deeps,
Blue as the overhanging heaven, that spread
And wind among the accumulated steeps;
A desert peopled by the storms alone,

Save when the eagle brings some hunter's bone,
And the wolf tracks her there – how hideously
Its shapes are heaped around! rude, bare, and high,
Ghastly, and scarred, and riven. – Is this the scene
Where the old Earthquake-daemon taught her young
Ruin? Were these their toys? or did a sea
Of fire envelop once this silent snow?
None can reply – all seems eternal now.
The wilderness has a mysterious tongue
Which teaches awful doubt, or faith so mild,
So solemn, so serene, that man may be,
But for such faith, with nature reconciled;
Thou hast a voice, great Mountain, to repeal
Large codes of fraud and woe; not understood
By all, but which the wise, and great, and good
Interpret, or make felt, or deeply feel.

IV

The fields, the lakes, the forests, and the streams,
Ocean, and all the living things that dwell
Within the daedal earth; lightning, and rain,
Earthquake, and fiery flood, and hurricane,
The torpor of the year when feeble dreams
Visit the hidden buds, or dreamless sleep
Holds every future leaf and flower; – the bound
With which from that detested trance they leap;
The works and ways of man, their death and birth,
And that of him, and all that his may be;
All things that move and breathe with toil and sound
Are born and die; revolve, subside, and swell.
Power dwells apart in its tranquility,
Remote, serene, and inaccessible:
And this, the naked countenance of earth,
On which I gaze, even these primaeval mountains

Teach the adverting mind. The glaciers creep
Like snakes that watch their prey, from their far fountains,
Slow rolling on; there, many a precipice,
Frost and the Sun in scorn of mortal power
Have piled: dome, pyramid, and pinnacle,
A city of death, distinct with many a tower
And wall impregnable of beaming ice.
Yet not a city, but a flood of ruin
Is there, that from the boundaries of the sky
Rolls its perpetual stream; vast pines are strewing
Its destined path, or in the mangled soil
Branchless and shattered stand; the rocks, drawn down
From yon remotest waste, have overthrown
The limits of the dead and living world,
Never to be reclaimed. The dwelling-place
Of insects, beasts, and birds, becomes its spoil;
Their food and their retreat for ever gone,
So much of life and joy is lost. The race
Of man flies far in dread; his work and dwelling
Vanish, like smoke before the tempest's stream,
And their place is not known. Below, vast caves
Shine in the rushing torrents' restless gleam,
Which from those secret chasms in tumult welling
Meet in the vale, and one majestic River,
The breath and blood of distant lands, for ever
Rolls its loud waters to the ocean-waves,
Breathes its swift vapours to the circling air.

v

Mont Blanc yet gleams on high: – the power is there,
The still and solemn power of many sights,
And many sounds, and much of life and death.
In the calm darkness of the moonless nights,
In the lone glare of day, the snows descend

Upon that Mountain; none beholds them there,
Nor when the flakes burn in the sinking sun,
Or the star-beams dart through them: — Winds contend
Silently there, and heap the snow with breath
Rapid and strong, but silently! Its home
The voiceless lightning in these solitudes
Keeps innocently, and like vapour broods
Over the snow. The secret Strength of things
Which governs thought, and to the infinite dome
Of Heaven is as a law, inhabits thee!
And what were thou, and earth, and stars, and sea,
If to the human mind's imaginings
Silence and solitude were vacancy?

With Mary beside Shelley as he wrote, echoes of this poem would find their way into *Frankenstein* too.

As if to emphasise his insistent godlessness, Shelley's hotel-register entry in Chamonix gave his profession (in Greek) as 'Democrat, Philanthropist and Atheist'; and if any doubt still remained, his family's destination was recorded as 'L'Enfer'.

Following a mid-August visit to Byron by 'Monk' Lewis, the Gothic novelist, poet and dramatist who had been unfortunately plagiarised just seven years earlier in Shelley's *Original Poetry by Victor and Cazire*, the inhabitants of the Maison Chappuis set off back to England, Shelley excitedly carrying book three of Byron's *Childe Harold's Pilgrimage*, Claire carrying a child (also Byron's).

Stopping at Versailles and Fontainbleau on their way, the family returned home, arriving on 8th September in London.

Even while I write,
my burning cheeks are wet...

Back in London, in the autumn of 1816, Shelley sent a copy of the *Hymn to Intellectual Beauty* anonymously to the radical journal editor and essayist Leigh Hunt, who agreed to publish it in his weekly *Examiner*. Shelley had first written to Hunt five years previously, and the men had met in person, but it was at around this time that their friendship really began in earnest.

Leigh Hunt lived with his family in the Vale of Health, in Hampstead, in a cottage which would become a second home to Shelley in the difficult coming months. Shelley met interesting people here, including Charles Ollier, who would soon become his publisher; Joseph Severn and the poet John Hamilton Reynolds; and William Hazlitt, with whom he argued politics, and who remembered Shelley as having 'a fire in his eye, a fever in his blood, a maggot in his brain, a hectic flutter in his speech, which mark out the philosophic fanatic...'

Here Shelley argued against religion (offending Benjamin Robert Haydon), and against monarchy (perhaps safer ground in this radical company), and with Hunt's son Thornton sailed paper boats on the Vale of Health pond.

When Hunt came to publish his *Young Poets*, a collection of writing by promising new voices, he would select three for inclusion – Shelley would be one, John Hamilton Reynolds the second, and the trio would be completed by the young, hugely talented John Keats. It was, of course, at the Hunts' that Shelley met Keats; he would come to be a great admirer of the younger poet's work, of his *Hyperion* especially. The two walked on Hampstead Heath, and Shelley, the wise elder (though himself still only 24) passed on advice about the dangers of publishing too soon. When the two men met, Keats – already showing evidence of an extraordinary gift – was still barely into his twenties.

So... Mary and Claire took lodgings at Bath, at 5 Abbey Churchyard, while Shelley visited Peacock at Marlow to organise the publication of some of Byron's work as a favour to his friend. At the end of September he rejoined the women in Bath.

An appalling few months would follow for Shelley and Mary. He had recently seen Fanny Imlay, Mary's half-sister (Mary Wollstonecraft's daughter by an earlier liaison), who now wrote him letters that caused him some alarm – she was unhappy and perhaps in love with him. News came on 9th October that she had committed suicide.

> *Her voice did quiver as we parted,*
> *Yet knew I not that heart was broken*
> *From which it came, and I departed*
> *Heeding not the words then spoken.*
> *Misery – O Misery,*
> *This world is all too wide for thee.*

Two months later, the second blow: Harriet, who until a couple of months earlier had been living in her father's London house on Chapel Street, was found dead in the Serpentine on 10th December. She too was believed to have taken her own life.

Three weeks later, at St Mildred's Church on Bread Street, Shelley and Mary Godwin were married.

The new year 1817 began with a huge and terrible unresolved question in Shelley's life – with Harriet dead, what would happen to their children, Ianthe and Charles? Though he barely knew them – he had hardly lived with Ianthe and never with Charles – Shelley was ready to fight for them. The hasty marriage to Mary – on the suggestion of Peacock – was intended to strengthen his case.

Just a week into January, Eliza and the Westbrooks filed a claim for their custody, citing as their reasons the father's irresponsibility, atheism, and the threat that the children might be exposed to seditious influence from which they ought really to be protected. Unfortunately for Shelley their claim was made to the Lord Chancellor Lord Eldon (formerly of University College, Oxford), who knew Shelley of old as a troublemaker. He deliberated on Westbrook v. Shelley, and came down in favour of the former. He did accept Shelley's proposal that rather than being adopted by the Westbrooks themselves the children be taken in by Dr and Mrs Hume, a decent couple outside the capital; but this was small consolation for another cruel blow to the now wretched Shelley.

Lines

I

The cold earth slept below,
Above the cold sky shone;
And all around, with a chilling sound,
From caves of ice and fields of snow,
The breath of night like death did flow
Beneath the sinking moon.

II

The wintry hedge was black,
The green grass was not seen,
The birds did rest on the bare thorn's breast,

Whose roots, beside the pathway track,
Had bound their folds o'er many a crack
Which the frost had made between.

III

Thine eyes glow'd in the glare
Of the moon's dying light;
As a fen-fire's beam on a sluggish stream
Gleams dimly, so the moon shone there,
And it yellow'd the strings of thy raven hair,
That shook in the wind of night.

IV

The moon made thy lips pale, belov'd –
The wind made thy bosom chill –
The night did shed on thy dear head
Its frozen dew, and thou didst lie
Where the bitter breath of the naked sky
Might visit thee at will.

By now the Shelleys had moved again, though not far afield – they were living now at Albion House, in Marlow, for which they had secured a 21-year lease. In early March, when Charles Ollier published Shelley's anonymous pamphlet on electoral reform, it was credited as being 'By the Hermit of Marlow'. As usual, copies were distributed hopefully among likely supporters.

Shelley knew Marlow already from his visits to his friend Peacock, and the house he found there now suited his needs very well. Albion House was a big neo-Gothic place, with five roomy bedrooms, as well as a nursery, a dining room, a large library and a study – enough to accommodate Shelley, Mary and baby William, Claire and her new baby (in January she had given birth to Byron's daughter, Allegra), and their modest staff – the children's governess, and so on.

Yes, Claire was again living with the family at Marlow; and to keep his stepsister-in-law happy, and encourage her in her musical accomplishments, Shelley bought her a piano at great expense (an expense, it's worth noting, that he was unable ever to meet). She was a captivating singer. Neighbour Thomas Love Peacock was one of those to fall in love with her, and remember her in his writing: she would contribute to the portrayal of Marionetta in his 1818 novel *Nightmare Abbey*. Shelley would write of her too, in particular in his piece inspired by her singing voice, 'To Constantia, Singing'.

I

Thus to be lost and thus to sink and die,
 Perchance were death indeed! – Constantia, turn!
In thy dark eyes a power like light doth lie,
 Even though the sounds which were thy voice, which burn
Between thy lips, are laid to sleep;
 Within thy breath, and on thy hair, like odour, it is yet,
And from thy touch like fire doth leap.
 Even while I write, my burning cheeks are wet.
 Alas, that the torn heart can bleed, but not forget!

II

A breathless awe, like the swift change
 Unseen, but felt in youthful slumbers,
Wild, sweet, but uncommunicably strange,
 Thou breathest now in fast ascending numbers.
The cope of heaven seems rent and cloven
 By the enchantment of thy strain,
And on my shoulders wings are woven,
 To follow its sublime career
Beyond the mighty moons that wane

Upon the verge of Nature's utmost sphere,
Till the world's shadowy walls are past and disappear.

III

Her voice is hovering o'er my soul – it lingers
  O'ershadowing it with soft and lulling wings,
The blood and life within those snowy fingers
  Teach witchcraft to the instrumental strings.
My brain is wild, my breath comes quick –
  The blood is listening in my frame,
And thronging shadows, fast and thick,
  Fall on my overflowing eyes;
My heart is quivering like a flame;
  As morning dew, that in the sunbeam dies,
  I am dissolved in these consuming ecstasies.

IV

I have no life, Constantia, now, but thee,
  Whilst, like the world-surrounding air, thy song
Flows on, and fills all things with melody. –
  Now is thy voice a tempest swift and strong,
On which, like one in trance upborne,
  Secure o'er rocks and waves I sweep,
Rejoicing like a cloud of morn.
  Now 'tis the breath of summer night,
Which when the starry waters sleep,
  Round western isles, with incense-blossoms bright,
  Lingering, suspends my soul in its voluptuous flight.

As at other Shelley homes, guests came and went – Hogg, Peacock, Godwin and Leigh Hunt. There were walks with friends to admire the surrounding nature in the extensive grounds and beyond; there was reading, talking about God and humanity, and boating on the Thames.

Mornings were spent writing – often afloat on the river – with one particular big project on the go. Leigh Hunt had set his friends Shelley and Keats a challenge – to produce a large narrative poetic work, with a six-month deadline. Keats set off on what would become *Endymion*, while Shelley worked on a major visionary piece of idealism and revolution set 'in Constantinople and modern Greece' (and an idealised version of the French Revolution), which he originally called *Laon and Cythna*. His mentor from Eton days, Dr James Lind, features in the story, as an old man who rescues Laon from imprisonment.

Though the preface suggests that this work should be easy to relate to, even for a reader today (less troubled by what might have been alarmingly cutting-edge two centuries ago) this twelve-canto piece begins with an introductory canto that is far from Shelley at his most accessible. But what it lacked in instant appreciability it certainly made up for in courage and provocativeness. This did not make it easy to publish, and once again the poet had to have it printed privately. When it finally came to be published by Ollier the following January, a number of the more provocative passages had to be excised – the incest, things like that... – with Ollier himself helping Shelley to wield the editorial knife. Even then, it only appeared unrecognisably hidden under a new title, *The Revolt of Islam*.

Thanks to some efforts on Shelley's part, a publisher had been secured for *Frankenstein*, and summer 1817 at Albion House saw Mary and Shelley reading the proofs, and Shelley writing a preface. The book was to be subtitled 'The Modern Prometheus'.

Mary was also preparing *History of a Six Weeks' Tour* for publication – this was a version of her and Shelley's travel journals of the 1814 European tour, which Hookham would publish this year. Shelley had contributed less and less to the journal as their trip progressed, but made up for it by his thoughtful, evocative and sometimes rapturous letters, through which all his travels would be assiduously recorded, and illuminated.

Here, for example, is that first sighting of Mont Blanc:

From Servoz three leagues remain to Chamouni – Mont Blanc was before us – the Alps, with their innumerable glaciers on high all around, closing in the complicated windings of the single vale – forests inexpressibly beautiful, but majestic in their beauty – intermingled beech and pine, and oak, overshadowed our road, or receded, whilst lawns of such verdure as I have never seen before, occupied these openings, and gradually became darker in their recesses. Mont Blanc was before us, but it was covered with cloud; its base, furrowed with dreadful gaps, was seen above. Pinnacles of snow intolerably bright, part of the chain connected with Mont Blanc, shone through the clouds at intervals on high. I never knew – I never imagined – what mountains were before. The immensity of these aerial summits excited, when they suddenly burst upon the sight, a sentiment of ecstatic wonder, not unallied to madness. And remember this was all one scene, it all pressed home to our regard and our imagination. Though it embraced a vast extent of space, the snowy pyramids which shot into the bright blue sky seemed to overhang our path; the ravine, clothed with gigantic pines, and black with its depth below, so deep that the very roaring of the untameable Arve, which rolled through it, could not be heard above – all was as much our own, as if we had been the creators of such impressions in the minds of others as now occupied our own. Nature was the poet, whose harmony held our spirits more breathless than that of the divinest.

Mary was pregnant again, and her daughter was born on 2nd September. She was called Clara Everina.

In November Princess Charlotte died, leading Shelley to write his 'Address to the People on the Death of Princess Charlotte'. While one might be surprised at such a subject for so ardent an anti-monarchist, all becomes clear on reading the pamphlet. For November had also seen the executions of three insurgents (a subject much more to Shelley's sympathies), and the pamphlet shows the author far more concerned with these individuals and what they meant for the country than with the death of a royal. 'The title,' wrote Medwin, 'was only a masque for politics. Under the lament of the Princess he typified Liberty, and rung her knell.'

Things may have seemed to be looking up after the previous appalling twelve months, but Shelley was not well, suffering from eye trouble, and what might have been consumption, too; and besides, the house was very damp. Perhaps they could go to Italy to help him recuperate? Byron was in Italy too, so such a trip would also allow them to reunite little Allegra with her wayward father. In December Albion House was put up for sale.

New Year's Day 1818 was the publication date of Mary's *Frankenstein*, which was reviewed in *The Quarterly Review*, unfavourably – to no surprise, as the periodical was a regularly unbalanced critic of Shelley too. *The Revolt of Islam* had fared particularly badly, the review describing its author as one who 'would overthrow the constitution, and then we should have no expensive court, no pensions or sinecures… no army or navy; he would pull down our churches, level our Establishment, and burn our bibles…'

Keats was another who would soon feel *The Quarterly*'s scorn, and would take it badly: Shelley believed this disillusionment had exacerbated his friend's illness, and would try to blame the reviewers for his premature death. Shelley, however, was getting almost used to such attitudes towards himself and his apparently dangerous work.

Lines to a Reviewer

Alas, good friend, what profit can you see
In hating such a hateless thing as me?
There is no sport in hate where all the rage
Is on one side: in vain would you assuage
Your frowns upon an unresisting smile,
In which not even contempt lurks to beguile
Your heart, by some faint sympathy of hate.
Oh, conquer what you cannot satiate:
For to your passion I am far more coy
Than even yet was coldest maid or boy
In winter noon. Of your antipathy
If I am the Narcissus, you are free
To pine into a sound with hating me.

In February 1818 the family left Albion House for a month in London. As far as we know Shelley did not visit his older children during this time, but spent his month doing things that better resembled a tourist's programme – seeing the sights, occasional visits to the opera, and so on. London these days had many Egyptian artefacts on show, and this public interest in – and access to – things Egyptian had recently led to what would be one of Shelley's best loved poems. Just a couple of months earlier he and his friend Horace Smith had agreed each to write a sonnet inspired by their visit to the recent discoveries displayed at the British Museum. Shelley would use it to present a theme dear to him: the limits of tyrannical power.

This is Shelley's *Ozymandias*:

I met a traveller from an antique land
Who said: Two vast and trunkless legs of stone
Stand in the desert... Near them, on the sand,
Half sunk, a shattered visage lies, whose frown,

And wrinkled lip, and sneer of cold command,
Tell that its sculptor well those passions read
Which yet survive, stamped on these lifeless things,
The hand that mocked them, and the heart that fed:
And on the pedestal these words appear:
'My name is Ozymandias, king of kings:
Look on my works, ye Mighty, and despair!'
Nothing beside remains. Round the decay
Of that colossal wreck, boundless and bare,
The lone and level sands stretch far away.

The three children in Shelley's household – William, Clara and their step-cousin Allegra – were christened at the church of St Giles in the Fields, in the West End of London, on 9th March. On the 10th the family said their goodbyes to Peacock, to Leigh Hunt and to Mary's ever-demanding father Godwin, and the following day they were off to Dover, and Italy. Shelley would not see England again.

Stanzas written in dejection...

From Calais, reached after a stormy Channel crossing, the party crossed France to Lyons, then over the Alps towards Italy. They were at Mont Cenis on 30th March, then went on to Susa and Turin, to Lake Como and Milan. 'We often hear of persons disappointed by a first visit to Italy,' Mary wrote later. 'This was not Shelley's case.'

Shelley liked Milan, visiting the opera, and sitting behind the altar in Milan Cathedral reading Dante. Throughout this time he continued to write regular letters to friends back home, producing a detailed and engaging set of pieces of narrative and description that assemble to give us a revealing picture of his experiences and his insights into the places he was visiting.

On 28th April, Allegra was introduced to her father, Lord Byron – she was sent over to Venice to meet him, accompanied by her nurse, Elise. The rest of the party went on to Pisa, and then Livorno.

Also at Livorno at this time were an English couple, John and Maria Gisborne. Shelley had arrived with an introduction from Godwin, who had long been a friend of Maria Gisborne (who had been in love with him – he had even proposed to her after Mary Wollstonecraft's death), and quickly befriended them. Mary appreciated the friendship, too – especially that of the woman who had once known her mother well – and it would significantly improve the Shelleys' experience of the place. It was thanks to Mrs Gisborne's Spanish lessons (which added to his already huge collection of languages) that Shelley was able to discover Calderón, a writer he would come to admire greatly. There was a little business arrangement attached to the agreeable friendship with this couple – Shelley schemed with Henry Reveley, Maria's son by a previous marriage, to set up a steamboat route to work the Mediterranean. (This would never actually happen. Obviously. Henry would two years later seek to persuade Claire to marry him, in which venture he would have equally little success.)

From a month appreciating the warm welcome of the Gisbornes at the Casa Ricci in Livorno, on now to Bagni di Lucca, the Casa Bertini, where the Shelley party (now with an added servant, Paolo) settled in June. The pattern of the two months spent here would have been familiar to anyone who knew Shelley – days made up of writing and reading (the scope of his reading lists, as recorded by Mary, is terrifying), of talking and taking long walks. He translated Plato's *Symposium* here, and worked on a new piece of writing, *Rosalind and Helen*, a 'modern eclogue' begun back in Marlow, which he had given up and now resumed at Mary's special request.

Around this time word reached the party from the governess Elise that all was not well with Allegra, who was living at Venice but not with her father. Shelley accompanied Claire via Florence to Venice, where they stopped off to see Allegra at the home of the British Consul. Shelley then went to speak with his friend about his rather inadequate parenting arrangements. The two poets went boating together, out to the Lido; then, thanks to certain good offices on Byron's part, an arrangement was made (rather out of the blue) to move Shelley and his entourage to a house at Este. Allegra's future had not been resolved to any-one's satisfaction, but she would at least be allowed to accompany her mother to the Este house, if only for a short visit.

Mary joined them from Lucca, but was troubled – baby Clara was sick, and was rushed to a doctor as soon as she had arrived in Venice, but in late September she died.

Shelley's *Lines Written Among the Euganean Hills* (the hills beside the house at Este) contains some echoes of the sadness this death provoked in him and in Mary. This is the opening:

Lines Written among
the Euganean Hills
October, 1818

Many a green isle needs must be
In the deep wide sea of Misery,
Or the mariner, worn and wan,
Never thus could voyage on –
Day and night, and night and day,
Drifting on his dreary way,
With the solid darkness black
Closing round his vessel's track;
Whilst above the sunless sky,
Big with clouds, hangs heavily,
And behind the tempest fleet
Hurries on with lightning feet,
Riving sail, and cord, and plank,
Till the ship has almost drank
Death from the o'er-brimming deep;
And sinks down, down, like that sleep
When the dreamer seems to be
Weltering through eternity;
And the dim low line before
Of a dark and distant shore
Still recedes, as ever still
Longing with divided will,
But no power to seek or shun,
He is ever drifted on
O'er the unreposing wave
To the haven of the grave.

What, if there no friends will greet;
What, if there no heart will meet
His with love's impatient beat;
Wander wheresoe'er he may,
Can he dream before that day
To find refuge from distress
In friendship's smile, in love's caress?
Then 'twill wreak him little woe
Whether such there be or no:
Senseless is the breast, and cold,
Which relenting love would fold;
Bloodless are the veins and chill
Which the pulse of pain did fill;
Every little living nerve
That from bitter words did swerve
Round the tortured lips and brow,
Are like sapless leaflets now
Frozen upon December's bough.

On the beach of a northern sea
Which tempests shake eternally,
As once the wretch there lay to sleep,
Lies a solitary heap,
One white skull and seven dry bones,
On the margin of the stones,
Where a few gray rushes stand,
Boundaries of the sea and land:
Nor is heard one voice of wail
But the sea-mews, as they sail
O'er the billows of the gale;
Or the whirlwind up and down
Howling, like a slaughtered town,
When a king in glory rides
Through the pomp of fratricides:
Those unburied bones around

There is many a mournful sound;
There is no lament for him,
Like a sunless vapour, dim,
Who once clothed with life and thought
What now moves nor murmurs not.

The poem also included an elegy to the brilliance of his friend Byron, of whom Shelley had become a huge admirer. Of *Don Juan*, he would write, 'Nothing has ever been written like it in English – nor if I may venture to prophesy, will there be.' And 'It sets him not only above, but far above, all the poets of the day – every word is stamped with immortality. I despair of rivalling Lord Byron, as well as I may, and there is no other with whom it is worth contending... It fulfils, in a certain degree, what I have long preached of producing – something wholly new and relative to the age, and yet surpassing beautiful...'

Shelley would soon begin another, very different kind of tribute to Byron, *Julian and Maddalo: a Conversation*, a narrative poem in rhyming couplets in which Julian and Count Maddalo tour Venice, sustaining as they go a long conversation on matters of importance (organised religion, predictably, being one of these). Shelley is Julian, but he is also the 'Maniac' whom Julian and Maddalo visit in the darkest section of the poem. Byron is drawn in the person of the Count, 'A person,' Shelley wrote in the Preface, 'of the most consummate genius, capable, if he would divert his energies to such an end, of becoming the redeemer of his degraded country.'

And there were, of course, more conventional tributes to his genius friend, too:

Sonnet to Byron

[I am afraid these verses will not please you, but]
If I esteemed you less, Envy would kill
Pleasure, and leave to Wonder and Despair
The ministration of the thoughts that fill
The mind which, like a worm whose life may share
A portion of the unapproachable,
Marks your creations rise as fast and fair
As perfect worlds at the Creator's will.
But such is my regard that nor your power
To soar above the heights where others [climb],
Nor fame, that shadow of the unborn hour
Cast from the envious future on the time,
Move one regret for his unhonoured name
Who dares these words: – the worm beneath the sod
May lift itself in homage of the God.

Allegra was returned to Byron in October, and the family was on the move again, leaving Este on 5th November and heading south – stopping first at Ferrara, visiting galleries in Bologna, then Rome. In Rome Shelley saw the Coliseum, and visited the Protestant cemetery, to which he took a liking. And from Rome to their intended final destination, Naples, a place they quickly came to love (even though Shelley had witnessed a murder soon after arriving).

Naples allowed Shelley to spend more time looking at art, to visit Pompeii and climb Vesuvius, and to finish the first act of his lyrical drama, *Prometheus Unbound*. But again Shelley was physically unwell, and unhappy too.

Stanzas Written in Dejection
Near Naples

I

The sun is warm, the sky is clear,
The waves are dancing fast and bright,
Blue isles and snowy mountains wear
The purple noon's transparent might,
The breath of the moist air is light,
Around its unexpanded buds;
Like many a voice of one delight,
The winds, the birds, the ocean floods,
The City's voice itself, is soft like Solitude's.

II

I see the Deep's untrampled floor
With green and purple seaweeds strown;
I see the waves upon the shore,
Like light dissolved in star-showers, thrown:
I sit upon the sands alone, –
The lightning of the noontide ocean
Is flashing round me, and a tone
Arises from its measured motion,
How sweet! did any heart now share in my emotion.

III

Alas! I have nor hope nor health,
Nor peace within nor calm around,
Nor that content surpassing wealth
The sage in meditation found,
And walked with inward glory crowned –
Nor fame, nor power, nor love, nor leisure.
Others I see whom these surround –

Smiling they live, and call life pleasure; –
To me that cup has been dealt in another measure.

IV

Yet now despair itself is mild,
Even as the winds and waters are;
I could lie down like a tired child,
And weep away the life of care
Which I have borne and yet must bear,
Till death like sleep might steal on me,
And I might feel in the warm air
My cheek grow cold, and hear the sea
Breathe o'er my dying brain its last monotony.

V

Some might lament that I were cold,
As I, when this sweet day is done,
Which my lost heart, too soon grown old,
Insults with this untimely moan;
They might lament – for I am one
Whom men love not, – and yet regret,
Unlike this day, which, when the sun
Shall on its stainless glory set,
Will linger, though enjoyed, like joy in memory yet.

For all the pleasures of Neapolitan tourism, there were domestic troubles in Naples, too. The Shelleys' servant, Paolo, who seems to have been a generally dishonest sort, managed to seduce the governess Elise, and the two were pressured by Shelley to marry. Early in the New Year Paolo would at last be fired, and he and Elise would leave the household. Meantime a scandal was born within the family, with the appearance on 27th December of a baby, christened Elena Adelaide Shelley, parents unspecified.

Elena was presumed by many to be not Shelley's adopted daughter, as might be suggested by her registered surname, but his illegitimate child; and with the help of the Gisbornes he certainly supported her. Some rumours claimed the baby girl was his child with Claire (a rumour that Byron heard and claimed to believe), others more credible that the mother was the governess Elise. Certainly the unscrupulous Paolo knew the truth, whatever it was, for the following summer he was trying to blackmail Shelley with the story of his 'Neapolitan charge'. By that time, though, the little girl in question was dead.

Shelley's visit to Pompeii in January 1819 was followed the next month by a few days in Paestum, and thence to Rome, where at Leigh Hunt's suggestion Amelia Curran would paint his portrait. It is this picture of the 26-year-old Shelley that provides the image of the poet – open-collared, rather feminine, tousle-haired, with that challenging look straight back at you – by which we recognise him today.

Rome would be home to the Shelleys for three months, which included the Easter festivities attended by the Emperor of Austria – Shelley himself would get over his many atheistic objections and his many republican objections for long enough to enjoy the revels. His tourism would include visits to St Peter's, and to the Caracalla baths; sitting on a hill above the baths he would finish acts two and three of *Prometheus Unbound*:

This Poem [explained its Preface] was chiefly written upon the mountainous ruins of the Baths of Caracalla, among the flowery glades, and thickets of odoriferous blossoming trees, which are extended in ever-winding labyrinths upon its immense platforms and dizzy arches suspended in the air. The bright blue sky of Rome, and the effect of the vigorous awakening of spring in that divinest climate, and the new life with which it drenches the spirits even to intoxication, were the inspiration of this drama.

Prometheus Unbound, for now a three-act drama (a fourth act would be written later, in Florence), depicts the conflict between Prometheus and Zeus, and the Titan's release from his bonds. It was a story Shelley knew from Aeschylus (whom he admired greatly), but where the old version evolves to a rather conciliatory resolution, Shelley spins the extra theme of the overthrowing of tyranny into his own. This work was, he considered, 'my best poem'.

Towards the end of spring, the Shelleys' boy, their lively little 'Willmouse', fell ill. On 7th June he died. He had lived a little over three years. On their previous visit to Rome Shelley had seen and loved the city's Protestant cemetery, and he returned there now, to bury his son.

To William Shelley

> *Thy little footsteps on the sands*
> *Of a remote and lonely shore;*
> *The twinkling of thine infant hands,*
> *Where now the worm will feed no more;*
> *Thy mingled look of love and glee*
> *When we returned to gaze on thee –*

The Shelleys had been contemplating a move from Rome in the summer anyway, but the death of William made this certain; days after his death they left the city, returning north to the countryside near Monte Nero, not far from Livorno, where they would be able to resume the company of the Gisbornes to help take their minds off their tragedy, and took the Villa Valsovano, a house with a little garden tower where Shelley could sit in sweltering summer heat and write.

To Mary Shelley

My dearest Mary, wherefore hast thou gone,
And left me in this dreary world alone?
Thy form is here indeed – a lovely one –
But thou art fled, gone down the dreary road,
That leads to Sorrow's most obscure abode;
Thou sittest on the hearth of pale despair,
                                                                      Where
For thine own sake I cannot follow thee.

The sad months at Livorno were in poetic terms among Shelley's most productive. He completed *Julian and Maddalo*, his Byron tribute. He also worked on his five-act blank verse tragedy *The Cenci*, based on a story he had been introduced to by Maria Gisborne, about Beatrice Cenci, whose portraits he had seen at the Colonna and Doria palaces, 'and her beauty cast the reflection of its own grace over her appalling story', Mary wrote. The play is an Elizabethan-style drama of the revenges and machinations that lead to the devastation of a Roman family. Shelley had the work printed and copies sent to Peacock to hawk anonymously around London theatres – this was (he hoped) a play for performance, not merely publication. To Mary, the fifth act was 'the finest thing he ever wrote'.

With his thoughts already turned homeward, Shelley was prompted by the Peterloo Massacre (in which fifteen people had been killed when the cavalry charged through a massive crowd of demonstrators who had assembled to demand parliamentary reform) to write his *Mask of Anarchy*, a fiercely political poem laying the blame for the massacre and the general state of the nation on its political leaders. It was written to be read not by these grandees, however, but by the working man, prompting him (so Shelley intended) to rise up – peacefully, of course – against their tyranny. To rise 'like lions after slumber / In unvanquishable number'. It is in ballad form, and the opening describes a sort of pageant of the worst culprits:

The Mask of Anarchy Written on the Occasion of the Massacre at Manchester

As I lay asleep in Italy
There came a voice from over the Sea,
And with great power it forth led me
To walk in the visions of Poesy.

I met Murder on the way –
He had a mask like Castlereagh –
Very smooth he looked, yet grim;
Seven blood-hounds followed him:

All were fat; and well they might
Be in admirable plight,
For one by one, and two by two,
He tossed them human hearts to chew
Which from his wide cloak he drew.

Next came Fraud, and he had on,
Like Eldon, an ermined gown;
His big tears, for he wept well,
Turned to mill-stones as they fell.

And the little children, who
Round his feet played to and fro,
Thinking every tear a gem,
Had their brains knocked out by them.

Clothed with the Bible, as with light,
And the shadows of the night,

Like Sidmouth, next, Hypocrisy
On a crocodile rode by.

And many more Destructions played
In this ghastly masquerade,
All disguised, even to the eyes,
Like Bishops, lawyers, peers, or spies.

Last came Anarchy: he rode
On a white horse, splashed with blood;
He was pale even to the lips,
Like Death in the Apocalypse.

And he wore a kingly crown;
And in his grasp a sceptre shone;
On his brow this mark I saw –
'I AM GOD, AND KING, AND LAW!'

With a pace stately and fast,
Over English land he passed,
Trampling to a mire of blood
The adoring multitude.

And a mighty troop around,
With their trampling shook the ground,
Waving each a bloody sword,
For the service of their Lord.

And with glorious triumph, they
Rode through England proud and gay,
Drunk as with intoxication
Of the wine of desolation.

O'er fields and towns, from sea to sea,
Passed the Pageant swift and free,

Tearing up, and trampling down;
Till they came to London town.

And each dweller, panic-stricken,
Felt his heart with terror sicken
Hearing the tempestuous cry
Of the triumph of Anarchy.

For with pomp to meet him came,
Clothed in arms like blood and flame,
The hired murderers, who did sing
'Thou art God, and Law, and King.

'We have waited, weak and lone
For thy coming, Mighty One!
Our purses are empty, our swords are cold,
Give us glory, and blood, and gold.'

Lawyers and priests, a motley crowd,
To the earth their pale brows bowed;
Like a bad prayer not over loud,
Whispering – 'Thou art Law and God.' –

Then all cried with one accord,
'Thou art King, and God, and Lord;
Anarchy, to thee we bow,
Be thy name made holy now!'

Shelley's old nemesis Lord Eldon – the man who had taken away the poet's children – cannot have been surprised to find himself featuring so explicitly in this piece...

'Shelley loved the People,' Mary would write, 'and respected them as often more virtuous, as always more suffering, and therefore more deserving of sympathy, than the great. He believed that a clash between the two classes of society was inevitable, and he eagerly ranged himself on the people's side.'

The unhappy goings-on back at home would also lead Shelley to write his 'Letter on Carlile', in support of the publisher Richard Carlile, who had brought trouble on himself by publishing writers like Thomas Paine and pirated works by Southey. They also inspired the sonnet 'England in 1819', in which he anatomises the state of the country with unusual bitterness, but typically finds a burst of optimism with which to end:

England in 1819

An old, mad, blind, despised, and dying king, –
Princes, the dregs of their dull race, who flow
Through public scorn, – mud from a muddy spring, –
Rulers who neither see, nor feel, nor know,
But leech-like to their fainting country cling,
Till they drop, blind in blood, without a blow, –
A people starved and stabbed in the untilled field, –
An army, which liberticide and prey
Makes as a two-edged sword to all who wield, –
Golden and sanguine laws which tempt and slay;
Religion Christless, Godless – a book sealed;
A Senate, – Time's worst statute unrepealed, –
Are graves, from which a glorious Phantom may
Burst, to illumine our tempestuous day.

Shelley's feelings about England cannot have been helped by the regular appearance in his and Mary's world of letters from her demanding father, insistently soliciting money; Shelley put the total he had given Godwin to date at a massive £4,700.

Thought-entangled descant...

The Shelleys' next home, where they moved in October, was Florence, the Palazzo Marini on the via Valfonda. Shelley was a regular visitor to the Uffizi, and continued his flurry of poetic production (including fine pieces on the art he saw there). Most notable of this time were two pieces, very different in their origins, their ambitions and executions.

First, a woodland walk along the Arno saw the birth of one of Shelley's best remembered poems, the 'Ode to the West Wind', in which the listless poet remembers the lost energy of his youth. And he compares his own flagging spirits to the endlessly energetic spirit of nature.

Ode to the West Wind

I

O wild West Wind, thou breath of Autumn's being,
Thou, from whose unseen presence of the leaves dead
Are driven, like ghosts from an enchanter fleeing,
Yellow, and black, and pale, and hectic red,
Pestilence-stricken multitudes: O thou,
Who chariotest to their dark wintry bed
The wingèd seeds, where they lie cold and low,

Each like a corpse within its grave, until
Thine azure sister of the Spring shall blow
Her clarion o'er the dreaming earth, and fill
(Driving sweet buds like flocks to feed in air)
With living hues and odours plain and hill:
Wild Spirit, which art moving everywhere;
Destroyer and preserver; hear, Oh, hear!

II

Thou on whose stream, mid the steep sky's commotion,
Loose clouds like earth's decaying leaves are shed,
Shook from the tangled boughs of Heaven and Ocean,
Angels of rain and lightning: there are spread
On the blue surface of thine aëry surge,
Like the bright hair uplifted from the head
Of some fierce Maenad, even from the dim verge
Of the horizon to the zenith's height,
The locks of the approaching storm. Thou dirge
Of the dying year, to which this closing night
Will be the dome of a vast sepulchre,
Vaulted with all thy congregated might
Of vapours, from whose solid atmosphere
Black rain, and fire, and hail will burst: Oh hear!

III

Thou who didst waken from his summer dreams
The blue Mediterranean, where he lay,
Lulled by the coil of his crystalline streams,
Beside a pumice isle in Baiae's bay,
And saw in sleep old palaces and towers
Quivering within the wave's intenser day,
All overgrown with azure moss and flowers
So sweet, the sense faints picturing them! Thou
For whose path the Atlantic's level powers

Cleave themselves into chasms, while far below
The sea-blooms and the oozy woods which wear
The sapless foliage of the ocean, know
Thy voice, and suddenly grow grey with fear,
And tremble and despoil themselves: Oh, hear!

IV

If I were a dead leaf thou mightest bear;
If I were a swift cloud to fly with thee;
A wave to pant beneath thy power, and share
The impulse of thy strength, only less free
Than thou, O uncontrollable! If even
I were as in my boyhood, and could be
The comrade of thy wanderings over Heaven,
As then, when to outstrip the skiey speed
Scarce seemed a vision; I would ne'er have striven
As thus with thee in prayer in my sore need.
Oh, lift me as a wave, a leaf, a cloud!
I fall upon the thorns of life! I bleed!
A heavy weight of hours has chained and bowed
One too like thee: tameless, and swift, and proud.

V

Make me thy lyre, even as the forest is:
What if my leaves are falling like its own!
The tumult of thy mighty harmonies
Will take from both a deep, autumnal tone,
Sweet though in sadness. Be thou, Spirit fierce,
My spirit! Be thou me, impetuous one!
Drive my dead thoughts over the universe
Like withered leaves to quicken a new birth!
And, by the incantation of this verse,
Scatter, as from an unextinguished hearth
Ashes and sparks, my words among mankind!

> *Be through my lips to unawakened earth*
> *The trumpet of a prophecy! O, Wind,*
> *If Winter comes, can Spring be far behind?*

Also written at some speed at this time was 'Peter Bell the Third', a parody of Wordsworth's recent poem 'Peter Bell, a Tale'; Shelley was unhappy with Wordsworth (who used to be such a good radical…), but this poem is a tribute to the best of Wordsworth, too. 'No man ever admired Wordsworth's poetry more,' wrote Mary; 'he read it perpetually, and taught others to appreciate its beauties…' Transcribed by a heavily pregnant Mary, 'Peter Bell the Third' was sent to Leigh Hunt, but it would not in fact be published for another twenty years.

In this poem, Peter travels through the grim underworld…

Peter Bell the Third
Part 3: Hell

> *Hell is a city much like London –*
> *A populous and a smoky city;*
> *There are all sorts of people undone,*
> *And there is little or no fun done;*
> *Small justice shown, and still less pity.*

> *There is a Castles, and a Canning,*
> *A Cobbett, and a Castlereagh;*
> *All sorts of caitiff corpses planning*
> *All sorts of cozening for trepanning*
> *Corpses less corrupt than they.*

> *There is a ***, who has lost*
> *His wits, or sold them, none knows which;*
> *He walks about a double ghost,*

And though as thin as Fraud almost –
    Ever grows more grim and rich.

There is a Chancery Court; a King;
    A manufacturing mob; a set
Of thieves who by themselves are sent
Similar thieves to represent;
    An army; and a public debt.

Which last is a scheme of paper money,
    And means – being interpreted –
'Bees, keep your wax – give us the honey,
And we will plant, while skies are sunny,
    Flowers, which in winter serve instead.'

There is a great talk of revolution –
    And a great chance of despotism –
German soldiers – camps – confusion –
Tumults – lotteries – rage – delusion –
    Gin – suicide – and methodism;

Taxes too, on wine and bread,
    And meat, and beer, and tea, and cheese,
From which those patriots pure are fed,
Who gorge before they reel to bed
    The tenfold essence of all these.

There are mincing women, mewing,
    (Like cats, who amant misère,)
Of their own virtue, and pursuing
Their gentler sisters to that ruin,
    Without which – what were chastity?

Lawyers – judges – old hobnobbers
    Are there – bailiffs – chancellors –

Bishops – great and little robbers –
Rhymesters – pamphleteers – stock-jobbers –
   Men of glory in the wars, –

Things whose trade is, over ladies
   To lean, and flirt, and stare, and simper,
Till all that is divine in woman
Grows cruel, courteous, smooth, inhuman,
   Crucified 'twixt a smile and whimper.

Thrusting, toiling, wailing, moiling,
   Frowning, preaching – such a riot!
Each with never-ceasing labour,
Whilst he thinks he cheats his neighbour,
   Cheating his own heart of quiet.

And all these meet at levees; –
   Dinners convivial and political; –
Suppers of epic poets; – teas,
Where small talk dies in agonies; –
   Breakfasts professional and critical;

Lunches and snacks so aldermanic
   That one would furnish forth ten dinners,
Where reigns a Cretan-tonguèd panic,
Lest news Russ, Dutch, or Alemannic
   Should make some losers, and some winners; –

At conversazioni – balls –
   Conventicles – and drawing-rooms –
Courts of law – committees – calls
Of a morning – clubs – book-stalls –
   Churches – masquerades – and tombs.

And this is Hell – and in this smother
    All are damnable and damned;
Each one damning, damns the other;
They are damned by one another,
    By none other are they damned.

'Tis a lie to say, 'God damns!'
    Where was Heaven's Attorney General
When they first gave out such flams?
Let there be an end of shams,
    They are mines of poisonous mineral.

Statesmen damn themselves to be
    Cursed; and lawyers damn their souls
To the auction of a fee;
Churchmen damn themselves to see
    God's sweet love in burning coals.

The rich are damned, beyond all cure,
    To taunt, and starve, and trample on
The weak and wretched; and the poor
Damn their broken hearts to endure
    Stripe on stripe, with groan on groan.

Sometimes the poor are damned indeed
    To take, – not means for being blessed, –
But Cobbett's snuff, revenge; that weed
From which the worms that it doth feed
    Squeeze less than they before possessed.

And some few, like we know who,
    Damned – but God alone knows why –
To believe their minds are given
To make this ugly Hell a Heaven;
    In which faith they live and die.

Thus, as in a town, plague-stricken,
   Each man be he sound or no
Must indifferently sicken;
As when day begins to thicken,
   None knows a pigeon from a crow, –

So good and bad, sane and mad,
   The oppressor and the oppressed;
Those who weep to see what others
Smile to inflict upon their brothers;
   Lovers, haters, worst and best;

All are damned – they breathe an air,
   Thick, infected, joy-dispelling:
Each pursues what seems most fair,
Mining like moles, through mind, and there
Scoop palace-caverns vast, where Care
In thronèd state is ever dwelling.

November was a good month, with an arrival that gave a much needed lift to the depressed spirits of the household. On the 12th a baby boy was born. He was christened Percy Florence Shelley; he was healthy, and would live.

But Shelley's own health was still compromised, so at the end of January the family moved again, taking a boat down the Arno to Pisa, where they settled at the Tre Donzelle inn.

Evening: Ponte al Mare, Pisa

I

The sun is set; the swallows are asleep;
    The bats are flitting fast in the grey air;
The slow soft toads out of damp corners creep,
    And evening's breath, wandering here and there
Over the quivering surface of the stream,
Wakes not one ripple from its summer dream.

II

There is no dew on the dry grass to-night,
    Nor damp within the shadow of the trees;
The wind is intermitting, dry, and light;
    And in the inconstant motion of the breeze
The dust and straws are driven up and down,
And whirled about the pavement of the town.

III

Within the surface of the fleeting river
    The wrinkled image of the city lay,
Immovably unquiet, and forever
    It trembles, but it never fades away;
Go to the …
You, being changed, will find it then as now.

IV

The chasm in which the sun has sunk is shut
    By darkest barriers of cinereous cloud,
Like mountain over mountain huddled – but
    Growing and moving upwards in a crowd,
And over it a space of watery blue,
Which the keen evening star is shining through.

Shelley liked Pisa. He made new friends – including the 'Masons', a couple whose real names were George Tighe and Lady Mountcashell, but who lived their liberated ex-pat lives together by the name of 'Mr and Mrs Mason' – and his good life here encouraged some fine writing, too. His 'Ode to Liberty' and 'The Sensitive Plant' (in which Mrs Mason would appear) date from this time; and he returned to his political passions, as he was bound always to do, with the long essay 'A Philosophical View of Reform', a brilliant piece of argument which would remain unpublished for a century. In it he wrote, 'Monarchy is only the string which ties the robber's bundle…'.

In some respects the most unusual and original of the poems of this time was 'The Cloud', in which a rain-cloud presents itself in the first person:

> I bring fresh showers for the thirsting flowers,
>   From the seas and the streams;
> I bear light shade for the leaves when laid
>   In their noonday dreams.
> From my wings are shaken the dews that waken
>   The sweet buds every one,
> When rocked to rest on their mother's breast,
>   As she dances about the sun.
> I wield the flail of the lashing hail,
>   And whiten the green plains under,
> And then again I dissolve it in rain,
>   And laugh as I pass in thunder.
>
> I sift the snow on the mountains below,
>   And their great pines groan aghast;
> And all the night 'tis my pillow white,
>   While I sleep in the arms of the blast.
> Sublime on the towers of my skiey bowers
>   Lightning my pilot sits;

In a cavern under is fettered the thunder,
    It struggles and howls at fits;
Over earth and ocean, with gentle motion,
    This pilot is guiding me,
Lured by the love of the genii that move
    In the depths of the purple sea;
Over the rills, and the crags, and the hills,
    Over the lakes and the plains,
Wherever he dream under mountain or stream
    The Spirit he loves remains;
And I all the while bask in Heaven's blue smile,
    Whilst he is dissolving in rains.

The sanguine Sunrise with his meteor eyes,
    And his burning plumes outspread,
Leaps on the back of my sailing rack,
    When the morning star shines dead;
As on the jag of a mountain crag,
    Which an earthquake rocks and swings,
An eagle alit one moment may sit
    In the light of its golden wings.
And, when Sunset may breathe, from the lit sea beneath,
    Its ardours of rest and of love,
And the crimson pall of eve may fall
    From the depth of Heaven above,
With wings folded I rest on mine aëry nest,
    As still as a brooding dove.

That orbèd maiden with white fire laden,
    Whom mortals call the Moon
Glides glimmering o'er my fleece-like floor,
    By the midnight breezes strewn;
And whenever the beat of her unseen feet,
    Which only the angels hear,
May have broken the woof of my tent's thin roof,

The stars peep behind her and peer;
And I laugh to see them whirl and flee,
    Like a swarm of golden bees,
When I widen the rent in my wind-built tent,
    Till the calm rivers, lakes, and seas,
Like strips of the sky fallen through me on high,
    Are each paved with the moon and these.

I bind the Sun's throne with a burning zone,
    And the Moon's with a girdle of pearl;
The volcanoes are dim, and the stars reel and swim,
    When the whirlwinds my banner unfurl.
From cape to cape, with a bridge-like shape,
    Over a torrent sea,
Sunbeam-proof, I hang like a roof, –
    The mountains its columns be.
The triumphal arch through which I march,
    With hurricane, fire, and snow,
When the Powers of the air are chained to my chair,
    Is the million-coloured bow;
The sphere-fire above its soft colours wove,
    While the moist Earth was laughing below.

I am the daughter of Earth and Water,
    And the nursling of the Sky;
I pass through the pores of the ocean and shores;
    I change, but I cannot die.
For after the rain when with never a stain
    The pavilion of heaven is bare,
And the winds and sunbeams with their convex gleams
    Build up the blue dome of air,
I silently laugh at my own cenotaph,
    And out of the caverns of rain,
Like a child from the womb, like a ghost from the tomb,
    I arise and unbuild it again.

From May the Gisbornes were spending a time back in England, and the Shelleys took up residence in their empty house near Livorno. From here, Shelley wrote his 'Letter to Maria Gisborne'. It is not a formal poem with a letter device as a conceit, but a real letter to a good friend – quite informal – which just happens to be a poem. A couple of passages by way of example:

>   ...*You are now*
> *In London, that great sea, whose ebb and flow*
> *At once is deaf and loud, and on the shore*
> *Vomits its wrecks, and still howls on for more.*
> *Yet in its depth what treasures! You will see*
> *That which was Godwin, – greater none than he*
> *Though fallen – and fallen on evil times – to stand*
> *Among the spirits of our age and land,*
> *Before the dread tribunal of to come*
> *The foremost, – while Rebuke cowers pale and dumb.*
> *You will see Coleridge – he who sits obscure*
> *In the exceeding lustre and the pure*
> *Intense irradiation of a mind,*
> *Which, with its own internal lightning blind,*
> *Flags wearily through darkness and despair –*
> *A cloud-encircled meteor of the air,*
> *A hooded eagle among blinking owls. –*
> *You will see Hunt – one of those happy souls*
> *Which are the salt of the earth, and without whom*
> *This world would smell like what it is – a tomb;*
> *Who is, what others seem; his room no doubt*
> *Is still adorned with many a cast from Shout,*
> *With graceful flowers tastefully placed about;*
> *And coronals of bay from ribbons hung,*
> *And brighter wreaths in neat disorder flung;*
> *The gifts of the most learned among some dozens*
> *Of female friends, sisters-in-law, and cousins.*
> *And there is he with his eternal puns,*

Which beat the dullest brain for smiles, like duns
Thundering for money at a poet's door;
Alas! it is no use to say, 'I'm poor!'
Or oft in graver mood, when he will look
Things wiser than were ever read in book,
Except in Shakespeare's wisest tenderness. –
You will see Hogg, – and I cannot express
His virtues, – though I know that they are great,
Because he locks, then barricades the gate
Within which they inhabit; – of his wit
And wisdom, you'll cry out when you are bit.
He is a pearl within an oyster shell.
One of the richest of the deep; – and there
Is English Peacock, with his mountain Fair,
Turned into a Flamingo; – that shy bird
That gleams i'the Indian air – have you not heard
When a man marries, dies, or turns Hindoo,
His best friends hear no more of him? – but you
Will see him, and will like him too, I hope,
With the milk-white Snowdonian Antelope
Matched with this cameleopard – his fine wit
Makes such a wound, the knife is lost in it;
A strain too learnèd for a shallow age,
Too wise for selfish bigots; let his page,
Which charms the chosen spirits of the time,
Fold itself up for the serener clime
Of years to come, and find its recompense
In that just expectation. – Wit and sense,
Virtue and human knowledge; all that might
Make this dull world a business of delight,
Are all combined in Horace Smith. – And these,
With some exceptions, which I need not tease
Your patience by descanting on, – are all
You and I know in London.
[…]

> *Next winter you must pass with me; I'll have*
> *My house by that time turned into a grave*
> *Of dead despondence and low-thoughted care,*
> *And all the dreams which our tormentors are;*
> *Oh! that Hunt, Hogg, Peacock, and Smith were there,*
> *With everything belonging to them fair! –*
> *We will have books, Spanish, Italian, Greek;*
> *And ask one week to make another week*
> *As like his father, as I'm unlike mine,*
> *Which is not his fault, as you may divine.*
> *Though we eat little flesh and drink no wine,*
> *Yet let's be merry: we'll have tea and toast;*
> *Custards for supper, and an endless host*
> *Of syllabubs and jellies and mince-pies,*
> *And other such lady-like luxuries, –*
> *Feasting on which we will philosophize!*
> *And we'll have fires out of the Grand Duke's wood,*
> *To thaw the six weeks' winter in our blood.*
> *And then we'll talk; – what shall we talk about?*
> *Oh! there are themes enough for many a bout*
> *Of thought-entangled descant; – as to nerves –*
> *With cones and parallelograms and curves*
> *I've sworn to strangle them if once they dare*
> *To bother me – when you are with me there.*
> *And they shall never more sip laudanum,*
> *From Helicon or Himeros; – well, come,*
> *And in despite of God and of the devil,*
> *We'll make our friendly philosophic revel*
> *Outlast the leafless time; till buds and flowers*
> *Warn the obscure inevitable hours,*
> *Sweet meeting by sad parting to renew; –*
> *'To-morrow to fresh woods and pastures new.'*

And this was not the best that came out of this brief sojourn. It was on a walk near this house, this summer, that Shelley heard the singing of a skylark. He wrote about it, about imagination, and about the process of creating poetry.

To a Skylark

Hail to thee, blithe Spirit!
Bird thou never wert,
That from Heaven, or near it,
Pourest thy full heart
In profuse strains of unpremeditated art.

Higher still and higher
From the earth thou springest
Like a cloud of fire;
The blue deep thou wingest,
And singing still dost soar, and soaring ever singest.

In the golden lightening
Of the sunken sun,
O'er which clouds are bright'ning,
Thou dost float and run;
Like an unbodied joy whose race is just begun.

The pale purple even
Melts around thy flight;
Like a star of Heaven,
In the broad daylight
Thou art unseen, but yet I hear thy shrill delight,

Keen as are the arrows
Of that silver sphere,
Whose intense lamp narrows
In the white dawn clear
Until we hardly see – we feel that it is there.

All the earth and air
　　With thy voice is loud,
As when night is bare,
　　From one lonely cloud
The moon rains out her beams, and Heaven is overflowed.

What thou art we know not;
　　What is most like thee?
From rainbow clouds there flow not
　　Drops so bright to see
As from thy presence showers a rain of melody.

Like a Poet hidden
　　In the light of thought,
Singing hymns unbidden,
　　Till the world is wrought
To sympathy with hopes and fears it heeded not:

Like a high-born maiden
　　In a palace-tower,
Soothing her love-laden
　　Soul in secret hour
With music sweet as love, which overflows her bower:

Like a glow-worm golden
　　In a dell of dew,
Scattering unbeholden
　　Its aëreal hue
Among the flowers and grass, which screen it from the view!

Like a rose embowered
　　In its own green leaves,
By warm winds deflower'd,
　　Till the scent it gives
Makes faint with too much sweet those heavy-wingèd thieves:

Sound of vernal showers
 On the twinkling grass,
Rain-awakened flowers,
 All that ever was
Joyous, and clear, and fresh, thy music doth surpass:

Teach us, Sprite or Bird,
 What sweet thoughts are thine:
I have never heard
 Praise of love or wine
That panted forth a flood of rapture so divine.

Chorus Hymeneal,
 Or triumphal chant,
Matched with thine would be all
 But an empty vaunt,
A thing wherein we feel there is some hidden want.

What objects are the fountains
 Of thy happy strain?
What fields, or waves, or mountains?
 What shapes of sky or plain?
What love of thine own kind? what ignorance of pain?

With thy clear keen joyance
 Languor cannot be:
Shadow of annoyance
 Never came near thee:
Thou lovest – but ne'er knew love's sad satiety.

Waking or asleep,
 Thou of death must deem
Things more true and deep
 Than we mortals dream,
Or how could thy notes flow in such a crystal stream?

We look before and after,
  And pine for what is not:
Our sincerest laughter
  With some pain is fraught;
Our sweetest songs are those that tell of saddest thought.

Yet if we could scorn
  Hate, and pride, and fear;
If we were things born
  Not to shed a tear,
I know not how thy joy we ever should come near.

Better than all measures
  Of delightful sound,
Better than all treasures
  That in books are found,
Thy skill to poet were, thou scorner of the ground!

Teach me half the gladness
  That thy brain must know;
Such harmonious madness
  From my lips would flow
The world should listen then – as I am listening now.

In August, while back in London Ollier was publishing *Prometheus Unbound* (to which a fourth and final act had been added in Florence), the Shelleys moved on to the spa town of San Giuliano, just a few miles outside Pisa. On a hot and tiring walk up to the chapel on the Monte San Pellegrino near Lucca on the 12th, Shelley devised his *Witch of Atlas*, a showy fantasy poem, written in *ottava rima* in just a few days. The 'Ode to Naples' would follow, and *Swellfoot the Tyrant*, a version of *Oedipus* which satirised the state of England and in particular the messy divorce proceedings of King George IV and

Queen Caroline. (Another work destined for anonymous publication, then.)

The origins of this latter piece are surely an inspiration unique in all literature. Shelley was reading his 'Ode to Liberty' to a visiting friend, fighting to be heard over the clamour of a fair taking place outside. The chorus of pigs grunting loudly outside the window prompted a comment from Shelley comparing them to Aristophanes' chorus of frogs. He then blithely postulated a silly satirical pseudo-tragedy whose chorus was made up of pigs; he wrote it, and *Swellfoot* was what emerged.

When *Prometheus Unbound* made it into print, it appeared attached to a collection of other short poems, which included the recent 'Ode to Liberty'.

from Ode to Liberty

XIII

England yet sleeps: was she not called of old?
    Spain calls her now, as with its thrilling thunder
Vesuvius wakens Aetna, and the cold
    Snow-crags by its reply are cloven in sunder:
O'er the lit waves every Aeolian isle
      From Pithecusa to Pelorus
      Howls, and leaps, and glares in chorus:
They cry, 'Be dim; ye lamps of Heaven suspended o'er us!'
    Her chains are threads of gold, she need but smile
      And they dissolve; but Spain's were links of steel,
    Till bit to dust by virtue's keenest file.
      Twins of a single destiny! appeal
To the eternal years enthroned before us
      In the dim West; impress us from a seal,
    All ye have thought and done! Time cannot dare conceal.

XIV

Tomb of Arminius! render up thy dead
*   Till, like a standard from a watch-tower's staff,*
His soul may stream over the tyrant's head;
*   Thy victory shall be his epitaph,*
Wild Bacchanal of truth's mysterious wine,
*   King-deluded Germany,*
*   His dead spirit lives in thee.*
Why do we fear or hope? thou art already free!
*   And thou, lost Paradise of this divine*
*   And glorious world! thou flowery wilderness!*
Thou island of eternity! thou shrine
*   Where Desolation, clothed with loveliness,*
Worships the thing thou wert! O Italy,
*   Gather thy blood into thy heart; repress*
*   The beasts who make their dens thy sacred palaces.*

Oh, that the free would stamp the impious name
*   Of KING into the dust! or write it there,*
So that this blot upon the page of fame
*   Were as a serpent's path, which the light air*
Erases, and the flat sands close behind!
*   Ye the oracle have heard:*
*   Lift the victory-flashing sword,*
And cut the snaky knots of this foul gordian word,
*   Which, weak itself as stubble, yet can bind*
*   Into a mass, irrefragably firm,*
*   The axes and the rods which awe mankind;*
*   The sound has poison in it, 'tis the sperm*
Of what makes life foul, cankerous, and abhorred;
*   Disdain not thou, at thine appointed term,*
*   To set thine armèd heel on this reluctant worm.*

Oh, that the wise from their bright minds would kindle
  Such lamps within the dome of this dim world,
That the pale name of PRIEST might shrink and dwindle
  Into the hell from which it first was hurled,
A scoff of impious pride from fiends impure;
    Till human thoughts might kneel alone,
    Each before the judgement-throne
Of its own aweless soul, or of the Power unknown!
  Oh, that the words which make the thoughts obscure
    From which they spring, as clouds of glimmering dew
From a white lake blot Heaven's blue portraiture,
    Were stripped of their thin masks and various hue
And frowns and smiles and splendours not their own,
    Till in the nakedness of false and true
    They stand before their Lord, each to receive its due! …

In the line about his name being trodden into the dust, the 'KING' was referred to discreetly as the '****'; but according to Blunden, when this piece was quoted in the consistently hostile *Quarterly Review* the '****' was replaced with '******', in the hope that readers might take it to be referring to Christ, and thus even more appalling than it already was…

Word reached Shelley this summer that John Keats was very sick. Keats was still in London, where his consumption had been steadily worsening – there had been haemorrhages, and coughing blood. Shelley wrote to encourage his friend to join him in Italy. But on arriving at Naples Keats and his friend Joseph Severn chose instead to travel to Rome, rather than venturing further north.

The flooding of the Baths of San Giuliano in late October would send the Shelleys back to Pisa; here they would meet Emilia

Viviani, a bright and spirited young woman kept hidden away in a convent, but who managed to get out occasionally to meet a lover, or to take walks with the nice English poet living nearby. Mary befriended Emilia too (though jealous of her husband's attentions), and they would all spend much time together in the early months of 1821. Emilia herself would spark off Shelley's 'Epipsychidion', which is addressed to 'the Noble and Unfortunate Lady Emilia V–, now imprisoned in the Convent of – ', and opens

> *Sweet Spirit! Sister of that orphan one,*
> *Whose empire is the name thou weepest on,*
> *In my heart's temple I suspend to thee*
> *These votive wreaths of withered memory.*

> *Poor captive bird! who, from thy narrow cage,*
> *Pourest such music, that it might assuage*
> *The ruggèd hearts of those who prisoned thee,*
> *Were they not deaf to all sweet melody;*
> *This song shall be thy rose: its petals pale*
> *Are dead, indeed, my adored Nightingale!*
> *But soft and fragrant is the faded blossom,*
> *And it has no thorn left to wound thy bosom…*

This poem, 'Epipsychidion', is Shelley's tribute to idealised love, which somehow manages to be simultaneously an entertaining advocation of free love, too…

> *Spouse! Sister! Angel! Pilot of the Fate*
> *Whose course has been so starless! O too late*
> *Belovèd! O too soon adored, by me!*
> *For in the fields of Immortality*
> *My spirit should at first have worshipped thine,*
> *A divine presence in a place divine;*
> *Or should have moved beside it on this earth,*

A shadow of that substance, from its birth;
But not as now: – I love thee; yes, I feel
That on the fountain of my heart a seal
Is set, to keep its waters pure and bright
For thee, since in those tears thou hast delight.
We – are we not formed, as notes of music are,
For one another, though dissimilar;
Such difference without discord, as can make
Those sweetest sounds, in which all spirits shake
As trembling leaves in a continuous air?

Thy wisdom speaks in me, and bids me dare
Beacon the rocks on which high hearts are wrecked.
I never was attached to that great sect,
Whose doctrine is, that each one should select
Out of the crowd a mistress or a friend,
And all the rest, though fair and wise, commend
To cold oblivion, though it is in the code
Of modern morals, and the beaten road
Which those poor slaves with weary footsteps tread,
Who travel to their home among the dead
By the broad highway of the world, and so
With one chained friend, perhaps a jealous foe,
The dreariest and the longest journey go.

Shelley sent 'Epipsychidion' to Ollier; this too he meant to be published anonymously – his name would attract only few friends' tributes anyway, and on balance very large numbers of enemies' attacks…

Emilia wasn't the only significant addition to Shelley's circle from this time; in January another English couple arrived at Pisa, who would play an important part in the closing chapters of Shelley's life: they were Edward and Jane Williams, and they arrived in Pisa in January.

Born in India, Edward Ellerker Williams had overlapped with Shelley at Eton, though as far as we know the two were not aware of each other there. Williams had grown into the role of a military man, and during an India posting had met and fallen for the unhappily married Jane Johnson. The two were soon living together as husband and wife, Jane going by the name of Mrs Williams though they never actually married.

In India Edward had befriended Tom Medwin, who told him of his cousin Shelley, inviting the Williamses to Europe to meet him. Edward Williams and Shelley were introduced in January 1821, and were firm friends from that first meeting. Shelley did not immediately feel any particular affection for Jane, but his feelings for her grew quickly in warmth, and before very long he would come to admire her greatly.

Sad news in late April. Shelley, accompanied by Williams and Reveley, had been down to Livorno to buy a boat, and decided to sail it back down to Pisa by canal. It capsized ('I nearly put an end to the Poet and myself,' Williams would write), and it fell to Reveley to play the hero and drag Shelley to shore – a lucky escape. The three were in good spirits when they reached Pisa, but arriving home Shelley found a letter from Leigh Hunt awaiting him. On 23rd February, Hunt reported, John Keats had died in Rome.

Though never a close friend or regular companion of Keats's, Shelley was one of the younger poet's greatest admirers, and was much moved at the news of his death, beginning at once to write his tribute, 'Adonais: An Elegy on the Death of John Keats'. This work, one of particular importance to Shelley himself, is about mortality and immortality – a magnificent 55-stanza tribute to a fellow poet and his work. It shows the influence of Milton, of Greek poets, and of the poems of Keats himself; and many other poets are given supporting parts, appearing in the poem to share in Shelley's tribute to his friend.

from Adonais:
An Elegy on the Death
of John Keats

I

I weep for Adonais – he is dead!
O, weep for Adonais! though our tears
Thaw not the frost which binds so dear a head!
And thou, sad Hour, selected from all years
To mourn our loss, rouse thy obscure compeers,
And teach them thine own sorrow, say: 'With me
Died Adonais; till the Future dares
Forget the Past, his fate and fame shall be
An echo and a light unto eternity!'

II

Where wert thou, mighty Mother, when he lay,
When thy Son lay, pierced by the shaft which flies
In darkness? where was lorn Urania
When Adonais died? With veilèd eyes,
'Mid listening Echoes, in her Paradise
She sate, while one, with soft enamoured breath,
Rekindled all the fading melodies,
With which, like flowers that mock the corse beneath,
He had adorn'd and hid the coming bulk of Death.

II

Oh, weep for Adonais – he is dead!
Wake, melancholy Mother, wake and weep!
Yet wherefore? Quench within their burning bed
Thy fiery tears, and let thy loud heart keep
Like his, a mute and uncomplaining sleep;
For he is gone, where all things wise and fair

Descend; – oh, dream not that the amorous Deep
Will yet restore him to the vital air;
Death feeds on his mute voice, and laughs at our despair.

IV

Most musical of mourners, weep again!
Lament anew, Urania! – He died,
Who was the Sire of an immortal strain,
Blind, old and lonely, when his country's pride,
The priest, the slave and the liberticide,
Trampled and mock'd with many a loathèd rite
Of lust and blood; he went, unterrified,
Into the gulf of death; but his clear Sprite
Yet reigns o'er earth; the third among the sons of light.

V

Most musical of mourners, weep anew!
Not all to that bright station dared to climb;
And happier they their happiness who knew,
Whose tapers yet burn through that night of time
In which suns perished; others more sublime,
Struck by the envious wrath of man or god,
Have sunk, extinct in their refulgent prime;
And some yet live, treading the thorny road,
Which leads, through toil and hate, to Fame's serene abode.

VI

But now, thy youngest, dearest one, has perished –
The nursling of thy widowhood, who grew,
Like a pale flower by some sad maiden cherish'd,
And fed with true-love tears, instead of dew;
Most musical of mourners, weep anew!
Thy extreme hope, the loveliest and the last,

> *The bloom, whose petals nipp'd before they blew*
> *Died on the promise of the fruit, is waste;*
> *The broken lily lies – the storm is overpast.*

VII

> *To that high Capital, where kingly Death*
> *Keeps his pale court in beauty and decay,*
> *He came; and bought, with price of purest breath,*
> *A grave among the eternal. – Come away!*
> *Haste, while the vault of blue Italian day*
> *Is yet his fitting charnel-roof! while still*
> *He lies, as if in dewy sleep he lay;*
> *Awake him not! surely he takes his fill*
> *Of deep and liquid rest, forgetful of all ill.*

VIII

> *He will awake no more, oh, never more! –*
> *Within the twilight chamber spreads apace*
> *The shadow of white Death, and at the door*
> *Invisible Corruption waits to trace*
> *His extreme way to her dim dwelling-place;*
> *The eternal Hunger sits, but pity and awe*
> *Soothe her pale rage, nor dares she to deface*
> *So fair a prey, till darkness and the law*
> *Of change shall o'er his sleep the mortal curtain draw.*

Keats was buried at Rome's Protestant cemetery, close to the grave of young William Shelley. In recognition of the fleetingness of life and renown, these words appear on his tombstone:

> This Grave contains all that was Mortal, of a young English Poet Who, on his Death Bed in the Bitterness of his heart at the Malicious Power of his enemies [that is, those nasty

reviewers], Desired these Words to be engraven on his Tomb Stone. Here lies One Whose Name was writ in Water.

XLVII

Who mourns for Adonais? Oh, come forth,
Fond wretch! and know thyself and him aright.
Clasp with thy panting soul the pendulous Earth;
As from a centre, dart thy spirit's light
Beyond all worlds, until its spacious might
Satiate the void circumference: then shrink
Even to a point within our day and night;
And keep thy heart light lest it make thee sink
When hope has kindled hope, and lured thee to the brink.

XLVIII

Or go to Rome, which is the sepulchre,
Oh, not of him, but of our joy: 'tis nought
That ages, empires, and religions there
Lie buried in the ravage they have wrought;
For such as he can lend, – they borrow not
Glory from those who made the world their prey;
And he is gathered to the kings of thought
Who waged contention with their time's decay,
And of the past are all that cannot pass away.

XLIX

Go thou to Rome, – at once the Paradise,
The grave, the city, and the wilderness;
And where its wrecks like shatter'd mountains rise,
And flowering weeds, and fragrant copses dress
The bones of Desolation's nakedness
Pass, till the spirit of the spot shall lead

Thy footsteps to a slope of green access
Where, like an infant's smile, over the dead
A light of laughing flowers along the grass is spread;

L

And gray walls moulder round, on which dull Time
Feeds, like slow fire upon a hoary brand;
And one keen pyramid with wedge sublime,
Pavilioning the dust of him who planned
This refuge for his memory, doth stand
Like flame transformed to marble; and beneath,
A field is spread, on which a newer band
Have pitched in Heaven's smile their camp of death,
Welcoming him we lose with scarce extinguished breath.

LI

Here pause: these graves are all too young as yet
To have outgrown the sorrow which consigned
Its charge to each; and if the seal is set,
Here, on one fountain of a mourning mind,
Break it not thou! too surely shalt thou find
Thine own well full, if thou returnest home,
Of tears and gall. From the world's bitter wind
Seek shelter in the shadow of the tomb.
What Adonais is, why fear we to become?

LII

The One remains, the many change and pass;
Heaven's light forever shines, Earth's shadows fly;
Life, like a dome of many-coloured glass,
Stains the white radiance of Eternity,
Until Death tramples it to fragments. – Die,
If thou wouldst be with that which thou dost seek!

Follow where all is fled! – Rome's azure sky,
Flowers, ruins, statues, music, words, are weak
The glory they transfuse with fitting truth to speak.

LIII

Why linger, why turn back, why shrink, my Heart?
Thy hopes are gone before: from all things here
They have departed; thou shouldst now depart!
A light is pass'd from the revolving year,
And man, and woman; and what still is dear
Attracts to crush, repels to make thee wither.
The soft sky smiles, the low wind whispers near:
'Tis Adonais calls! oh, hasten thither,
No more let Life divide what Death can join together.

LIV

That Light whose smile kindles the Universe,
That Beauty in which all things work and move,
That Benediction which the eclipsing Curse
Of birth can quench not, that sustaining Love
Which through the web of being blindly wove
By man and beast and earth and air and sea,
Burns bright or dim, as each are mirrors of
The fire for which all thirst; now beams on me,
Consuming the last clouds of cold mortality.

LV

The breath whose might I have invok'd in song
Descends on me; my spirit's bark is driven,
Far from the shore, far from the trembling throng
Whose sails were never to the tempest given;
The massy earth and spherèd skies are riven!
I am borne darkly, fearfully, afar;

> *Whilst, burning through the inmost veil of Heaven,*
> *The soul of Adonais, like a star,*
> *Beacons from the abode where the Eternal are.*

Just over a year from now, this final stanza would show an eerie prescience for Shelley's own story.

For all Shelley's pride in it, the poem had only a mixed response; some friends liked it, but the published version was barely remarked upon. After 'Adonais' he contemplated writing more on Keats – publishing a critical essay, a memoir of the poet with a collection of Keats's writings – but not much came of these plans. It may be that he would have come to write these planned works in time, had he himself lived longer. But as spring 1821 turned to summer, he was entering his own final year.

Our boat is asleep…

So 1821 was of the year of 'Adonais', one of Shelley's most enduring works; but he wrote much else besides.

Peacock had lately published his 'Four Ages of Poetry', a semi-serious essay arguing for the increasing irrelevance of poetry in a developed society, and Shelley was this spring moved to write a response: 'The Defence of Poetry'. Though he had recorded his thoughts on poetry many times before, usually in prefaces published appended to his poems, this bold and insightful essay was the most sustained and coherent argument. And it builds to an ending on a note of something like triumph:

> It is impossible to read the compositions of the most celebrated writers of the present day without being startled with the electric life which burns within their words. They measure the circumference and sound the depths of human nature with a comprehensive and all penetrating spirit, and they are themselves perhaps the most sincerely astonished at its manifestations: for it is less their spirit than the spirit of the age. Poets are the hierophants of an unapprehended inspiration; the mirrors of the gigantic shadows which futurity casts upon the present; the words which express what they understand not; the trumpets which sing to battle and feel not what they inspire; the influence which is moved not, but moves. Poets are the unacknowledged legislators of the world.

Then there were initial thoughts towards a new English tragedy: 'Charles the First', which he would not finish. And 'Hellas', a dramatic poem advocating the cause of liberty in Greece, written in response to the War of Independence raging since March, and which following his meeting the Greek prince Alexander Mavrocordato Shelley watched at a distance from his peaceful Tuscan oasis. This too ends with a song of optimism – 'The world's great age begins anew, / The golden years return...'

'If such a poem becomes popular,' wrote Williams, 'we may flatter ourselves of having advanced a step towards improvement and perfection in all things, moral and political.'

There was plenty of leisure time this summer too, of course. On one summer's day Shelley took the boat out with Edward Williams again. He wrote a poem, 'The Boat on the Serchio':

from The Boat on the Serchio

Our boat is asleep on Serchio's stream,
Its sails are folded like thoughts in a dream,
The helm sways idly, hither and thither;
    Dominic, the boatman, has brought the mast,
    And the oars, and the sails; but 'tis sleeping fast,
Like a beast, unconscious of its tether.

The stars burnt out in the pale blue air,
And the thin white moon lay withering there;
To tower, and cavern, and rift, and tree,
The owl and the bat fled drowsily.
Day had kindled the dewy woods,
    And the rocks above and the stream below,
And the vapours in their multitudes,
    And the Apennines' shroud of summer snow,
And clothed with light of aëry gold

The mists in their eastern caves uprolled.
Day had awakened all things that be,
The lark and the thrush and the swallow free,
    And the milkmaid's song and the mower's scythe
And the matin-bell and the mountain bee:
Fireflies were quenched on the dewy corn,
    Glow-worms went out on the river's brim,
    Like lamps which a student forgets to trim:
The beetle forgot to wind his horn,
    The crickets were still in the meadow and hill:
Like a flock of rooks at a farmer's gun
Night's dreams and terrors, every one,
Fled from the brains which are their prey
From the lamp's death to the morning ray...

In August Shelley travelled over to Ravenna to visit Byron. He stopped to see Allegra in her convent home; he heard – delighted – Byron read Canto V of *Don Juan*; Byron told him of the rumours circulating about the Shelley family arrangements (in particular about the alleged illegitimate child with Claire); and Shelley made plans for his friend to move to Pisa, which Byron duly did in November.

So by November the Pisa circle has significantly expanded. Shelley is back here now, and Byron has moved into a nearby Pisan palace, the Casa Lanfranchi. The Williamses have returned to Pisa, too, after some months living at nearby Pugnano, and move into the ground floor of the Tre Palazzi di Chiesa, the building on the Lung'Arno in which the Shelleys had taken upper-floor rooms. Their friend Tom Medwin visits this same month, and is most excited to have cousin Shelley introduce him to the infamous Lord Byron. Medwin would sit late into the night just listening to the poets talk, taking notes in a diary for some future use...

'It was not until he spoke that you could discern anything uncommon in him,' another friend would write of Shelley, 'but the first sentence he uttered, when excited by his subject, riveted your attention. The light from his very soul streamed from his eyes, and every emotion of which the human mind is susceptible, was expressed in his pliant and ever-changing features.'

And another group of visitors is expected to arrive before too long, too: Leigh Hunt and his family. Hunt, writing from Hampstead, had lately been in touch with Shelley to discuss the possibility of the two of them and Byron collaborating to set up a new periodical – originally intended to be called *Hesperides* – and planned a trip to Italy to visit his friends and discuss the necessary arrangements. When the Hunts arrived the plan was for them to be put up in the ground floor of Byron's palatial home. They were expected towards the end of the year.

But there was no sign of them as Christmas approached. (Christmas Day was marked by a bet between Byron and Shelley on which of them would gain his inheritance first – with the first inheritor to pay a thousand pounds to the other. In the event Byron's mother-in-law would die obligingly within a matter of weeks, but he seems not to have paid up.) The weather over the Christmas period was rough, as Williams recorded in his journal: 'Violent wind, with wind [sic] and sleet. A hat having blown into the river, a poor fellow volunteered to fetch it in a small boat, but was almost instantly carried down by a whirlpool, and neither man nor boat have since been heard of.'

Ill weather had delayed the Hunts in their intended journey, too, and they had not yet arrived when the new year began. It was 1822.

While the wait for Leigh Hunt continued, another addition to the circle appeared in early 1822. This was Edward John

Trelawny, a man with a taste for adventure and a very impressive moustache. A former naval officer, he had met Williams and Medwin at Geneva; Williams invited him to Pisa, and there introduced him to Shelley, and Shelley introduced him to Byron. (Trelawny had already read and admired both.) Though something of a fantasist – keen to promote the image of himself as romantic hero – Trelawny's accounts are a surprisingly reliable source for the events of the following months. Among other entertainments during this time, Trelawny once tried to teach Shelley to swim:

> I was bathing one day in a deep pool in the Arno, and astonished the Poet by performing a series of aquatic gymnastics, which I had learnt from the natives of the South Seas. On my coming out, whilst dressing, Shelley said mournfully,
>
> 'Why can't I swim, it seems so very easy?'
>
> I answered, 'Because you think you can't. If you determine, you will; take a header off this bank, and when you rise turn on your back, you will float like a duck... '
>
> He doffed his jacket and trowsers, kicked off his shoes and socks, and plunged in, and there he lay stretched out on the bottom like a conger eel, not making the least effort or struggle to save himself. He would have been drowned if I had not instantly fished him out...

But this particular pastime was not pursued with much eagerness, as there were many other more dramatic calls on the company's attention. On 18th February, Williams wrote in his diary, 'Called on Lord B., who talks of getting up Othello.' For the group had come up with the notion of a bit of amateur dramatics, putting on a production of the Shakespeare tragedy with Shelley directing, Trelawny in the title role, Byron as Iago and Mary the unfortunate Desdemona, Edward and Jane Williams as Cassio and Emilia, Medwin as Roderigo. Despite the initial enthusiasm, this good idea did not develop far...

But there was plenty else. There was lively and intelligent debate ('Shelley's mental activity was infectious,' wrote Trelawny; 'he kept your brain in constant action'). There was excitement in the form of a fray between an English shooting party (Byron, Shelley, Trelawny and others) and an Italian dragoon who was severely wounded. But more often entertainment was calmer – domestic, pleasant, friendly, as Williams wrote of this more typical day:

'Sunday, February 24th. Fine. Claire calls. Wrote some lines. Read my first act to Medwin. Call on Lord B., beat him at billiards, and played till evening with Trelawny. The S.'s, M., and T. dine here.'

Literary production was storming ahead in the Pisa circle these days. In 1822, Byron published his *Cain*. Shelley translated parts of *Faust*, and walking in the forests near Pisa was moved to write two poems for Jane Williams, 'Recollection' and 'Invitation'. She would be remembered in others of his works of this time too, including this famous lyric:

To Jane: 'The keen stars were twinkling'

I

The keen stars were twinkling,
And the fair moon was rising among them,
Dear Jane!
The guitar was tinkling,
But the notes were not sweet till you sung them
Again.

II

As the moon's soft splendour
O'er the faint cold starlight of Heaven
Is thrown,

So your voice most tender
To the strings without soul had then given
Its own.

III

The stars will awaken,
Though the moon sleep a full hour later,
To-night;
No leaf will be shaken
Whilst the dews of your melody scatter
Delight.

IV

Though the sound overpowers,
Sing again, with your dear voice revealing
A tone
Of some world far from ours,
Where music and moonlight and feeling
Are one.

By April the Shelleys were ready to move to a summer residence, away from Byron and closer to the open sea that Shelley loved so much. Claire was sent with the Williamses as a scouting party to try and find a house further up the coast on the Bay of Spezia. (During their little excursion, Williams would write, rather endearingly, in his journal entry for the 22nd, 'My birthday. Forget whether born in 1793 or 1794 – rather think the former.')

No sooner had Claire left Pisa than Shelley received word that on the 19th, four days earlier, her daughter Allegra had succumbed to typhus fever and died at the convent in Bagnacavallo. Shelley delayed telling Claire till he had got her away from Byron and settled at their new home. On 30th April the Shelley-Clairmont-Williams party moved into the Casa Magni at San

Terenzo, near Lerici on the Bay of Spezia. 'Poor Claire' – wrote Williams – 'quite unconscious of the burden on her friends' minds.' But on the evening of 1st May, the day after the move, she accidentally walked in on Shelley and Williams in anxious conversation, and guessed that her daughter was dead.

The Casa Magni was an isolated house right by the water, a house that better suited Shelley's taste for solitude than it did Mary's constant wish for company. Their marriage was cooler than it had ever been before.

For Shelley it was a perfect setting, especially once his new toy had arrived; for he and Byron had commissioned a friend of Trelawny's, Captain Daniel Roberts, to build them each a boat. Shelley's arrived on 12th May and he and Williams began to use it at once. 'We have now a perfect plaything for the summer,' wrote Williams. Shelley had meant to call his new boat *Ariel*, but Byron beat him to it and gave it the name *Don Juan*, naming his own, which arrived the following day (with Trelawny and Roberts as crew), the *Bolivar*.

The boat, the setting, the presence of his friend Williams, these all helped Shelley's mood. But his work had begun to demoralise him – not the work itself, so much as his publishing troubles, and the difficulty in finding success and a decent-sized, appreciative audience with what little he was able to get widely published. Mary wrote:

Shelley did not expect sympathy and approbation from the public, but the want of it took away a portion of the ardour that ought to have sustained him while writing. He was thrown on his own resources, and on the inspiration of his own soul; and wrote because his mind overflowed, without the hope of being appreciated... if his poems were more addressed to the common feelings of men, his proper rank among writers of the day would be acknowledged, and that popularity as a poet would enable his countrymen to do justice to his character and virtues, which in those days it was the mode to attack with the most flagitious calumnies and insulting abuse.

> *Alas! this is not what I thought life was.*
> *I knew that there were crimes and evil men,*
> *Misery and hate; nor did I hope to pass*
> *Untouched by suffering, through the rugged glen.*
> *In mine own heart I saw as in a glass*
> *The hearts of others   And when*
> *I went among my kind, with triple brass*
> *Of calm endurance my weak breast I armed,*
> *To bear scorn, fear, and hate, a woful mass!*

And then another family tragedy struck. Mary had been pregnant when the family moved into the Casa Magni, but on 16th June suffered a dangerous miscarriage and was only saved by Shelley's emergency ministrations. The miscarriage, following as it did the deaths of three of her children, as well as Allegra and Elena – five children of the household in seven years – was devastating. For Mary the devastation was physical as well as emotional – she had lost a lot of blood, and was left fragile, and vulnerable.

On 13th June, at long last, the Hunts arrived at Genoa. From there they travelled to Livorno; Shelley would enjoy sailing down the Ligurian coast in the little *Don Juan* to meet them. (That this was open sea rather than a lake or a well-sheltered bay seems not to have given Shelley any pause at all.) Stopping at Lerici to pick up Roberts, Shelley and Williams crewed the little boat from the Casa Magni down to Livorno on Monday 1st July. They arrived that night, and Shelley and Hunt were reunited the following morning. The old friends hadn't seen each other for four years, and the reunion was most touching, as Hunt would later recall.

The Hunts did now move into the ground floor of the Casa Lanfranchi (as had been planned the previous year), though things were strained with Byron, who was suddenly less keen on the idea of collaborating on the proposed new periodical (the title of which had by now changed from *Hesperides* to *The Liberal*). Hunt had money troubles, which were only aggravated by Byron's coolness towards his plans to get the new scheme underway.

On the 3rd and 4th, Williams would write his final diary entries:

Wednesday, July 3. Fine, strong sea-breeze.

Thursday, July 4. Fine. Processions of priests and religiosi have for several days been active in their prayers for rain; but the gods are either angry or nature is too powerful.

By Sunday 7th July it was time for Shelley and Williams to return home. Shelley borrowed fifty pounds from Byron; he borrowed a copy of Keats's *Hyperion* from Hunt to read on the return journey (having misplaced his own); and he and Williams returned to the dock at Livorno. Having secured the services of Charles Vivian, an eighteen-year-old English boat-boy, they set off for home the following day. There was a good wind as Roberts and Trelawny watched the *Don Juan* pull away from Livorno to head north along the open coast. Trelawny followed her progress through his spyglass, until his friends had disappeared from view.

Those eyes where once hope shone...

Mutability

I

The flower that smiles to-day
*   To-morrow dies;*
All that we wish to stay
*   Tempts and then flies.*
What is this world's delight?
Lightning that mocks the night,
*   Brief even as bright.*

II

Virtue, how frail it is!
*   Friendship how rare!*
Love, how it sells poor bliss
*   For proud despair!*
But we, though soon they fall,
Survive their joy, and all
*   Which ours we call.*

Whilst skies are blue and bright,
  Whilst flowers are gay,
Whilst eyes that change ere night
  Make glad the day;
Whilst yet the calm hours creep,
Dream thou – and from thy sleep
  Then wake to weep.

More than a week after the storm had come and gone, the bodies floated up to the surface of the water, and drifted slowly to land. Williams was the first to appear, on the 17th – almost unrecognisable, but for a boot, and a black silk handkerchief around his neck, monogrammed 'E.E.W.'. With him was his journal, which has helped us as an important record of Shelley's final days – it has a sketch Williams had made of his friend, too.

Epitaph

These are two friends whose lives were undivided;
So let their memory be, now they have glided
Under the grave; let not their bones be parted,
For their two hearts in life were single-hearted.

On the 18th, Shelley's body was washed ashore near Viareggio – he too had been wasted almost beyond recognition by his time in the water. He had Hunt's copy of Keats in his pocket, folded open.

'The spell snapped;' wrote Mary, 'it was all over; an interval of agonising doubt – of days passed in miserable journeys to gain tidings, of hopes that took firmer root even as they were more baseless – was changed to the certainty of the death that eclipsed all happiness for the survivors for evermore.'

The news reached the press back in London on 4th August, which would have been Shelley's thirtieth birthday. *The Courier* reported, 'Shelley, the writer of some infidel poetry has been drowned; *now* he knows whether there is a God or no.'

In early August Byron wrote to his friend and publisher John Murray:

> I presume you have heard that Mr Shelley & Capt. Williams were lost on the 7th [sic] Ulto. in their passage from Leghorn to Spezia in their own open boat. You may imagine the state of their families. – I never saw such a scene – nor wish to see such another. – You are all brutally mistaken about Shelley who was without exception – the *best* and least selfish man I ever knew. – I never knew one who was not a beast in comparison.

Quarantine laws meant that the bodies had to be buried quickly, but Trelawny later managed to secure permission to have them dug up for cremation. Both Shelley and Williams were cremated near Viareggio, Williams on 15th August and Shelley the following day, the latter laid on the pyre with the copy of Keats he had been reading in his final hours. Byron, Hunt and a group of curious locals looked on.

Trelawny gives an account of the sad proceedings of exhuming and cremating his friend's body:

> Three white wands had been stuck in the sand to mark the Poet's grave, but as they were at some distance from each other, we had to cut a trench thirty yards in length, in the line of the sticks, to ascertain the exact spot, and it was nearly an hour before we came upon the grave.

In the meantime Byron and Leigh Hunt arrived in the carriage, attended by soldiers, and the Health Officer, as before. The lonely and grand scenery that surrounded us so exactly harmonised with Shelley's genius, that I could imagine his spirit soaring over us. The sea, with the islands of Gorgona, Capraji, and Elba, was before us; old battlemented watch-towers stretched along the coast, backed by the marble-crested Apennines glistening in the sun, picturesque from their diversified outlines, and not a human dwelling in sight. As I thought of the delight Shelley felt in such scenes of loneliness and grandeur whilst living, I felt we were no better than a herd of wolves or a pack of wild dogs, in tearing out his battered and naked body from the pure yellow sand that lay so lightly over it, to drag him back to the light of day; but the dead have no voice, nor had I power to check the sacrilege – the work went on silently in the deep and unresisting sand, not a word was spoken, for the Italians have a touch of sentiment, and their feelings are easily excited into sympathy. Even Byron was silent and thoughtful. We were startled and drawn together by a dull hollow sound that followed the blow of a mattock; the iron had struck a skull, and the body was soon uncovered. Lime had been strewn on it; this, or decomposition, had the effect of staining it of a dark and ghastly indigo colour. Byron asked me to preserve the skull for him; but remembering that he had formerly used one as a drinking-cup, I was determined Shelley's should not be so profaned. The limbs did not separate from the trunk, as in the case of Williams's body, so that the corpse was removed entire into the furnace. I had taken the precaution of having more and larger pieces of timber, in consequence of my experience of the day before of the difficulty of consuming a corpse in the open air with our apparatus. After the fire was well kindled we repeated the ceremony of the previous day; and more wine was poured over Shelley's dead body than he had consumed during his life. This with the oil and salt made the yellow flames glisten and quiver. The heat from the sun and fire was so intense that the atmosphere was tremulous and wavy. The corpse fell open and the heart was laid bare. The frontal bone of the skull, where it had been struck with the mattock, fell off; and, as the back of the head rested on the red-hot bottom bars of the furnace, the brains literally seethed, bubbled, and boiled as in a cauldron, for a very long time.

Byron could not face this scene, he withdrew to the beach and swam off to the *Bolivar*. Leigh Hunt remained in the carriage. The fire was so fierce as to produce a white heat on the iron, and to reduce its contents to grey ashes. The only portions that were not consumed were some fragments of bones, the jaw, and the skull, but what surprised us all, was that the heart remained entire.

Trelawny burned his hand badly while seeking to retrieve his friend's heart from the embers.

In April 1823, with Trelawny once more taking care of arrangements, Shelley's ashes were taken to the Protestant Cemetery in Rome, and buried in an isolated spot beside the old wall. Trelawny chose some words from *The Tempest* for the stone:

> *Nothing of him that doth fade*
> *But doth suffer a sea-change*
> *Into something rich and strange.*

Above it, the Latin inscription, *Cor cordium* – Heart of hearts.

Jane Williams took Edward's ashes back to London, where they were set at Kensal Green Cemetery. A few years later she settled down with Hogg (keen as ever to please himself according to Shelley's own tastes), living with him until his death in 1862.

In 1823, with Shelley's ashes now resting with their son in Rome, Mary returned to England. She would not marry again, living the rest of her life as Shelley's widow.

That same year Shelley's two older children left the home of the Humes, Ianthe going to her aunt Eliza (who now became her legal guardian – which would have appalled Shelley) and Charles to his grandfather Timothy (which Shelley would not have liked all that much either). Timothy arranged a good education for his grandson, which mirrored that which he had provided for his eldest son, Bysshe – though presum-ably hoping for a different result this time; first Charles went to the local school at Warnham, where the Reverend Evan Edwards was still teaching, and then on to Syon House. But in 1826 he died of consumption, and was buried in St Margaret's church, Warnham. The stone (in what is now the vestry) describes him only as 'grandson of Sir Timothy and Lady Elizabeth Shelley'.

Percy Bysshe Shelley, the boy's father, is not mentioned. But lest his own name risked being – like Keats' ominous warning – 'writ in water', his friends (each for his own reason good or ill) would not let the poet's story be forgotten. Each felt his own version of that story ought to be told.

In 1857 Hogg – at the request of Sir Percy Shelley, the son – would write his *Life of Shelley*, assembled with access to the family papers. It is a biased account of only dubious accuracy, which depicts Shelley as rather unhinged, a madcap and a fant-asist and the author himself as his constant supporter, his loyal mentor. It has a tendency to over-dramatise, and a tendency too to forget that it is supposed to be a book about Shelley, so interested is it in Hogg himself. Shelley's poetry hardly receives a mention, and it is not surprising that these volumes were pub-lished to the considerable dismay of the family. (Though, how-ever unreliable, it's often pleasingly anecdotal and remains a useful source for the earlier years, before many of his other biographers knew him.)

Tom Medwin had a few Shelley books and articles in him too, inevitably; having kept a diary of his time in Italy with his cousin and friends, he published *Conversations with Lord Byron*, a little *Memoir of Percy Bysshe Shelley* in 1833 and in 1847 the two-volume *Life of Percy Bysshe Shelley*, far from a hundred per cent accurate but at least less obviously partisan than Hogg's offering.

Hogg's accuracy would be questioned by Trelawny, who published his own *Recollections of the Last Days of Shelley and Byron* in 1858. Trelawny was infinitely sympathetic to Shelley's views – the more radical the better – and his biography is kinder to his friend than Hogg's. Trelawny's own story would continue to be entwined with his friend's in a possibly surprising fashion. In 1828 he proposed to Mary, who said no; and then he tried proposing to Claire (with whom he might have had a brief affair) who said no, too. He had been married and divorced twice already, and would be again. In 1881 he would die in Sussex, and his ashes brought to Rome to be buried next to his friend, with the 'Epitaph' penned by Shelley (see p. 134) on his tombstone.

And Shelley survives in Peacock's pen, too, portrayed as Scythrop in *Nightmare Abbey*, troubled with a 'passion for reforming the world', who 'built many castles in the air', an affectionate satire which he lived to see (a copy was sent to him in Italy) and which pleased him.

Mary worked for the rest of her life to secure for posterity her husband's writing, and in particular the poems whose collected publication she would herself supervise. The *Poetical Works*, which would include her notes on the poems and the life of the poet (from which most of her words quoted in this book are taken) appeared in 1839.

Mary herself died in 1851 and is buried at St Peter's church, Bournemouth. With her are her parents, and Shelley's heart rescued from the pyre by Trelawny. (Some have suggested the probability that it was in fact his liver, not his heart, that would have burned last, but that rather takes away from the Romantic symbolism…)

In 1894 a marble memorial statue of the drowned Shelley by sculptor Onslow Ford was unveiled in Oxford, at University College, where he had spent those few inglorious months. This curious rehabilitation came more than seven decades after his death.

Though critically unappreciated, Shelley's influence was great in his own lifetime, of course – on Mary's *Frankenstein*, say, and on the work of his friend Byron. But his influence on the poets who followed him was just as great – on the Victorians, Browning (in particular), Tennyson and Swinburne, and on through Yeats and beyond.

Bernard Shaw, a fellow vegetarian, 'regretted that Shelley's artistic excellence, now beyond question, overshadowed his importance as a leader of thought'. He was admired by Karl Marx. The Chartist movement for reform in the 1830s was influenced by his writings, and 'Queen Mab' came to be known as 'the Chartists' Bible'. He was set to music by Rakhmaninov and Elgar, he was played by Julian Sands in a Ken Russell film, and he appeared in the third series of *Blackadder*.

And it continues today. A search for 'Shelley' and 'poetry' on Google offers close to four million results. These include a doctoral thesis examining his influence on the non-violent movements of Gandhi and Martin Luther King; and an 'I ❤ Percy Bysshe Shelley' mug ($9.99); and a New Yorker cartoon in which a workman's head appears through a manhole in the middle of some Manhattan roadworks saying 'My name is Ozymandias, king of kings; Look on my works, ye Mighty, and despair…'.

Early in his final year Shelley had started work on his great visionary poem 'The Triumph of Life', much of it written on the water, 'as he sailed or weltered on that sea which was soon to engulf him', Mary wrote. In it the Chariot of Life is seen to be a destructive force, an enemy to idealism, crushing all human hope…

'Before the chariot had begun to climb
The opposing steep of that mysterious dell,
Behold a wonder worthy of the rhyme

'Of him who from the lowest depths of hell,
Through every paradise and through all glory,
Love led serene, and who returned to tell

'The words of hate and awe; the wondrous story
How all things are transfigured except Love;
For deaf as is a sea, which wrath makes hoary,

'The world can hear not the sweet notes that move
The sphere whose light is melody to lovers –
A wonder worthy of his rhyme. – The grove

'Grew dense with shadows to its inmost covers,
The earth was gray with phantoms, and the air
Was peopled with dim forms, as when there hovers

'A flock of vampire-bats before the glare
Of the tropic sun, bringing, ere evening,
Strange night upon some Indian isle; thus were

'Phantoms diffused around; and some did fling
Shadows of shadows, yet unlike themselves,
Behind them; some like eaglets on the wing

'Were lost in the white day; others like elves
Danced in a thousand unimagined shapes
Upon the sunny streams and grassy shelves;

'And others sate chattering like restless apes
On vulgar hands, …
Some made a cradle of the ermined capes

'Of kingly mantles; some across the tiar
Of pontiffs sate like vultures; others played
Under the crown which girt with empire

'A baby's or an idiot's brow, and made
Their nests in it. The old anatomies
Sate hatching their bare broods under the shade

'Of daemon wings, and laughed from their dead eyes
To reassume the delegated power,
Arrayed in which those worms did monarchize,

'Who made this earth their charnel. Others more
Humble, like falcons, sate upon the fist
Of common men, and round their heads did soar;

'Or like small gnats and flies, as thick as mist
On evening marshes, thronged about the brow
Of lawyers, statesmen, priest and theorist; –

'And others, like discoloured flakes of snow
On fairest bosoms and the sunniest hair,
Fell, and were melted by the youthful glow

'Which they extinguished; and, like tears, they were
A veil to those from whose faint lids they rained
In drops of sorrow. I became aware

'Of whence those forms proceeded which thus stained
The track in which we moved. After brief space,
From every form the beauty slowly waned;

'From every firmest limb and fairest face
The strength and freshness fell like dust, and left
The action and the shape without the grace

'Of life. The marble brow of youth was cleft
With care; and in those eyes where once hope shone,
Desire, like a lioness bereft

'Of her last cub, glared ere it died; each one
Of that great crowd sent forth incessantly
These shadows, numerous as the dead leaves blown

'In autumn evening from a poplar tree.
Each like himself and like each other were
At first; but some distorted seemed to be

'Obscure clouds, moulded by the casual air;
And of this stuff the car's creative ray
Wrought all the busy phantoms that were there,

'As the sun shapes the clouds; thus on the way
Mask after mask fell from the countenance
And form of all; and long before the day

'Was old, the joy which waked like heaven's glance
The sleepers in the oblivious valley, died;
And some grew weary of the ghastly dance,

'And fell, as I have fallen, by the wayside; –
Those soonest from whose forms most shadows passed,
And least of strength and beauty did abide.

'Then, what is life? I said… the cripple cast
His eye upon the car of beams which now had rolled
Onward, as if that look must be the last

'And answered… 'Happy those for whom the fold
Of

And so it would end, unfinished.

For this final work, a piece much influenced by the writers of his adopted Italy (his 'paradise of exiles', he called it), politics, society and monarchy had all been sidelined in favour of simple humanity. Because it is unfinished, we do not know whether the conclusion was to have been pessimistic or redemptive. But it seems from what we know of Shelley – the insistent improver of the world – that the latter is more likely.

Shelley died before turning thirty, a cruelly short life. But a life into which so much had been crammed – so much creativity and passion and curiosity, so much experience and tragedy. In his last days, at Livorno with the Hunts, he had commented that even if he were to die the next day he would have lived longer than his grandfather – returning to the ideas of a note in *Queen Mab* in which he had observed the differences between a richly intellectual, questioning life and an empty one: 'The life of a man of virtue and talent, who should die in his thirtieth year, is, with regard to his own feelings, longer than that of a miserable priest-ridden slave, who dreams out a century of dullness.'

Not long after *Queen Mab*, when he was perhaps twenty years old, Shelley had written these words:

> *Dark flood of Time,*
> *Roll as it listeth thee: I measure not*
> *By months or moments thy ambiguous course.*
> *Another may stand by me on thy brink*
> *And watch the bubble whirled beyond his ken*
> *Which pauses at my feet.   The sense of love,*
> *The thirst for action, and the impassioned thought*
> *Prolong my being; if I wake no more,*
> *My life more actual living will contain*
> *Than some gray veteran's of the world's cold school,*
> *Whose listless hours unprofitably roll,*
> *By one enthusiast feeling unredeemed,*

Virtue and Love! unbending Fortitude,
Freedom, Devotedness and Purity!
That life my Spirit consecrates to you.

No one could say that Shelley's own life lacked 'enthusiast feeling'; by his own measure, a brief life well worth living.

List of works

The dates given in brackets correspond to the (sometimes approximate) date of composition.

The text of the poems reproduced in this book has been taken from Thomas Hutchinson's Oxford edition of 1905.

Further reading

It has been more than a little troublesome to select the few offerings of Shelley's poetry that could fit into an introductory volume of this size. So the first piece of further reading to encourage must be a more leisurely browse through the complete poems, in particular some of the longer works which for reasons of space have had to be neglected here. The standard edition for almost a century was *Shelley's Poetical Works*, edited by Thomas Hutchinson, first published in 1905 and subsequently revised and reprinted a number of times. With only occasional exceptions, the poems quoted in this volume are given as they appear in Hutchinson. The letters are taken from the Roger Ingpen edition of 1909 (the standard edition now is probably the two-volume F.L. Jones edition of 1964). The Wordsworth Poetry Library selection of Shelley edited by Bruce Woodcock includes most of the prose you might want to read.

For the biographies there are first all those many contributions by friends of the poet, which I've described above. And then of course very many others more recent, far too many to mention. So just a few of the more unusual ones...

André Maurois's *Ariel* is a reasonably mad sort of 'romance', with foolish dialogue and bits of novelistic character ('...Hogg heaved a sigh and lifted his eyebrows...') and of very little use as biography but extremely entertaining. Largely disregarded now, Edmund Blunden's *Shelley* is a favourite of mine (but that's just me, I realise) – often partisan, sometimes utterly peculiar, but a frequently brilliant and always charming, sympathetic read. Ann Wroe's *Becoming Shelley* is a reconstruction of Shelley the poet – rather than Shelley the man; a marvellously creative book about a creative soul, a life told 'inside out'. And Paul Foot's *Red Shelley* is unique, a brilliant and odd unpacking of Shelley's politics as found in his writing.

But none of these comes close to Richard Holmes's *Shelley: the Pursuit*. Comprehensive, sympathetic, insightful – head and shoulders above anything anyone else has written about Shelley; it hasn't been surpassed in its thirty-five years of life to date, and (as Shelley so confidently predicted of *Don Juan*) never will be. So read that.

Then go back and read those poems again.

Acknowledgments

A few thank-yous. To Abi, for enduring a long morning's patient punctuating; to Tom Harding, himself a descendent of Shelley's, for some information on the poet's grandchildren; to Richard Holmes, for writing *Shelley: a Pursuit*, always the gold standard; to the British Library and the London Library, where all the answers are; to Jenny Rayner and everyone at Hesperus for commissioning this book, and in particular to Ellie Robins for guiding it from manuscript to book with both efficiency and imagination; to my mother, who read it first; and to Tanweena and Mehran and their friends, who amid all the mayhem in Cornwall just let me get on with it.

Shelley lived by a very special, very particular combination of general optimism and specific doubt; writing about him often made me think of Chester, who has just the same qualities, I think. (I hope he agrees.) So this book is dedicated to him.

Biographical note

Daniel Hahn is a writer, editor and translator. Most notable among the reference books he has co-edited have been the 'Ultimate Book Guides', an award-winning series of reading guides for children and teenagers; his translations include the autobiography of Brazilian footballer Pelé. He works regularly with Shakespeare's Globe, and is on the international council of Human Rights Watch, as well as being associated with a number of other organisations that promote translation, literacy and freedom of expression, of which he hopes Shelley might have approved. He lives in Brighton, so he passes through Shelley's birthplace on the train almost every day. He is thirty-five years old.